# GREAT LIVES OBSERVED

Gerald Emanuel Stearn, *General Editor*

EACH VOLUME IN THE SERIES VIEWS THE CHARACTER AND
ACHIEVEMENT OF A GREAT WORLD FIGURE IN THREE PER-
SPECTIVES—THROUGH HIS OWN WORDS, THROUGH THE OPIN-
IONS OF HIS CONTEMPORARIES, AND THROUGH RETROSPECTIVE
JUDGMENTS—THUS COMBINING THE INTIMACY OF AUTOBIOG-
RAPHY, THE IMMEDIACY OF EYEWITNESS OBSERVATION, AND
THE OBJECTIVITY OF MODERN SCHOLARSHIP.

MORTON BORDEN, *coeditor of this volume in the Great Lives
Observed series, is Professor of History at the University of
California, Santa Barbara. He has published widely on the
early national period of American history, including a previous
volume in the series,* George Washington.

PENN BORDEN, *coeditor, received her B.A. and M.A. degrees in
history from the University of Montana, but was persuaded to
leave an academic career to become the wife and intellectual
helpmate of Dr. Borden.*

GREAT LIVES OBSERVED

# THE AMERICAN TORY

GREAT LIVES OBSERVED

# THE *American Tory*

# Edited by MORTON BORDEN and PENN BORDEN

*If America is the happier for the revolution,
I declare solemnly that I shall rejoice
that the side I was on was the unsuccessful one.*

—PETER VAN SCHAACK

A SPECTRUM BOOK

PRENTICE-HALL, INC., ENGLEWOOD CLIFFS, N.J.

PRENTICE-HALL INTERNATIONAL, INC. (*London*)
PRENTICE-HALL OF AUSTRALIA, PTY. LTD. (*Sydney*)
PRENTICE-HALL OF CANADA, LTD. (*Toronto*)
PRENTICE-HALL OF INDIA PRIVATE LIMITED (*New Delhi*)
PRENTICE-HALL OF JAPAN, INC. (*Tokyo*)

*For all the Torgenruds*

# Contents

## PART ONE
## AMERICAN TORIES LOOK AT THE WORLD

### 1
### Tory Arguments Upholding Law and Order      14

Letter from a Virginian, 1774, *14*    Samuel Seabury's Address, 1774, *16*    Jabez Fisher of Pennsylvania, 1774, *18* A Tory pasquinade of the New York rebels, 1774, *19* William Eddis of Maryland, 1775, *21*    Governor William Franklin's letter to the New Jersey legislature, 1776, *23* Peter Oliver's account, 1776, *24*    Reverend Charles Inglis, 1777, *25*

### 2
### Tory Experiences in Revolutionary America      27

Letter of Reverend Samuel Peters, having fled from Connecticut to Boston, 1774, *27*    Letter of Ann Hulton from Boston, 1774, *27*    Intimidating an old Tory, 1775, *29* The proselytization of a Rhode Island Tory, 1775, *30* Daniel Coxe to Cortland Skinner, Attorney General of New Jersey, 1775, *31*    Account of the Rev. Jonathan Boucher, 1775, *31*    Samuel Curwen of Salem flees to Philadelphia, 1775, *34*    A Philadelphia Tory suggests that England use more military force, 1776, *36*    Governor James Wright of Georgia asks for military assistance, 1776, *37*    The bravery of a Maryland Tory described in

# 6

## The Problem of Controlling Tories in Wartime    78

Brigadier-General John Sullivan to George Washington, 1775, *78*  Henry Fisher to the Committee of Safety in Delaware, October, 1776, *78*  A loyalty oath for suspected Tories in Rhode Island, 1776, *79*  Applying the loyalty oath on Long Island, 1776, *80*  Proceedings of the General Assembly held for the Colony of Rhode Island, July, 1776, *80*  Washington's proclamation, 1777, *81*  The advice of Samuel Adams, 1777, *82*  Robert R. Livingston, Matthew Cantine and Zephaniah Platt to the President of the Provincial Convention of New York, 1777, *83*  Colonel William Richardson to the Commissioners of the Board of War in Philadelphia, 1777, *84*  An act more effectively to prevent the mischiefs, arising from the influence and example of persons of equivocal and suspected characters, in this state [New York]. Passed the 30th of June, 1778, *84*  Minutes of the Commissioners for Detecting and Defeating Conspiracies in the state of New York: Albany County Sessions, 1778–1781, *87*  The conviction and penalty of Seagoe Potter for treason in Delaware, 1780, *89*

# 7

## Postwar Attitudes Toward Tories          91

John Jay to Peter Van Schaack, 1782, *91*  Rebel feeling in New York: two letters and a newspaper item, 1783, *92*  The rebel poet, Philip Freneau, writes a Tory's epistle upon his departure for Nova Scotia, 1783, *93*  Aedanus Burke of South Carolina, 1783, *96*  Benjamin Franklin: who was more loyal to America, 1785, *97*  Benjamin Franklin: analysis of the loyalists, 1788, *98*

## PART THREE
## HISTORICAL APPRAISALS OF THE AMERICAN TORIES

David Ramsay: A Rebel View of the Revolution, *100*
Thomas Jones: A Tory View of the Revolution, *105*

GREAT LIVES OBSERVED

# THE AMERICAN TORY

# Introduction

Tori.

The conservative is by nature fearful. He risks only when confronted with no other alternative. He has courage, but only to face the known. He cannot project that courage into the future. In short, the conservative lacks daring and foresight; he holds, instead, an ability to innovate only within the narrow confines of the status quo. Conservatives are admired; but only those who dare are idolized, at least, those who dare successfully.

The American Tory has borne a double burden of historical and popular disapproval, since he could not envision future greatness as a separate nation and was long judged and condemned as unpatriotic. He espoused a political philosophy that was grounded in tradition, in stable law, and long-polished justice. His arguments were, in more cases than not, well-reasoned, erudite, and ponderous with precedent. But the question must be asked: when must uncertain change take precedence over established belief? To the Tory mind gradual change was the utopian way; swift transition led only to chaos, anarchy, and the displacement, forever, of classical beauty. To his mind present evil was to be borne stoically, for a future grounded in tradition would erase his suffering. He could not see that such gradualism frequently results in complacency. Tradition very often loses its humanity and tries to find fulfillment in security.

Tories came from all classes, but many were of the intellectual elite who had a suspicion of common democracy. To be administered well, they believed, government must be composed of men competent to govern, and such men were found only in the upper class. Would not a revolution spew up uneducated leaders of an undisciplined following, demagogues with no sense of the past and little concern for the future? The Tories believed their political position was unassailable, based as it was on calm reason and dispassionate judgment, the fruit of their education and social position. The decision to remain loyal stemmed from long, hard scrutiny, close examination through logic, and reasoned argument. It was not that they loved America less, but, inbred as it was in them, they could not go against what they most deeply believed. Their beliefs were

1

not arrived at lightly. In exile, Peter Van Schaack attempted to explain this in-depth soul-searching:

> With respect to the great contest in which, unfortunately, I differed
> from others of my valuable friends as well as yourself, I can say with
> the most sacred regard to truth, I was actuated by no motive un-
> friendly to my country, nor by any consideration of a personal
> private nature. Men's hearts are not always known, even to them-
> selves; but, believe me that I spared no pains in examining into
> all the secret recesses of mine . . . and if America is happier for the
> revolution, I declare solemnly that I shall rejoice that the side I
> was on was the unsuccessful one.

The great question they all labored over was how much can be suffered before violent overthrow is justified? To those Tories who prided themselves on thoughtful and truthful analysis, the colonial complaints were legitimate, and corrections were needed; some came almost to the line of rebellion, as did Peter Van Schaack. But in the end they could not justify violence as a remedy. Evils were present, but reform through laws and through established procedure was the only honorable and justifiable alternative. Laws were to be obeyed. If they were bad laws, they must be amended, but as long as they remained, they *must be obeyed*. The Navigation Acts were thought, by many Tories, to be improper laws. Thomas Hutchinson did not approve of the Stamp Act but he felt that its repeal would also be "admitting their [America's] principle of total independence." Hutchinson further maintained that "he ever thought the taxing America by Parliament not advisable," but as a servant of the Crown, "I thought myself bound to discountenance the violent opposition made to the Act, as it led to the denial of its authority in all cases whatsoever, and in fact, had brought on the rebellion."

James Allen, the son of one of the "great families" of Pennsylvania, believed King George III to be "as despotic as any prince in Europe." But he too wrestled with the dilemma of reconciling reason with revolt. Devoted to the cause of liberty, he could not shed his faith in the British constitution. "I love the Cause of Liberty," wrote Allen, "but cannot heartily join in the prosecution of measures totally foreign to the original plan of Resistance. The madness of the multitude is but one degree better than submission to the Tea-Act."

Honorable men differed. Tories and rebels arrayed their evidence before the public. Each attempted to prove, either by historical and constitutional precedents, or by appeals to reason and natural law, or by philosophical arguments, or by polemical outbursts, the rightness of his cause. Peter Van Schaack, Thomas Hutchinson, and James Allen could not pass that line from protest into rebellion. Thomas Jefferson, John Adams, and Benjamin Franklin did. If both could prove their cases, then the essence of their differences lay in the one question: were present evils sufferable? To the Tories they were. To the rebels it seemed clear that present evils would only lead to greater ones. Rebellion was deadly serious; not to be taken except for grave cause. But rebellion, as Thomas Jefferson in the Declaration of Independence concluded, was the last answer to injustice suffered too long:

> Prudence, indeed, will dictate that governments long established should not be changed for light and transient causes; and, accordingly, all experience hath shown, that mankind are more disposed to suffer, while evils are sufferable, than to right themselves by abolishing the forms to which they are accustomed. But, when a long train of abuses and usurpations, pursuing invariably the same Object, evinces a design to reduce them under absolute Despotism, it is their right, it is their duty, to throw off such Government, and to provide new Guards for their future Security.

Thus the distinction between rebel and Tory became hardened as rebellion became imminent. The best of the Tories, who loved their country as much as the rebels, were deemed traitors as well as those who remained loyal for meaner reasons. All Tories were treated as criminals, whether their motives were noble or ignoble. In crude war, finer distinctions are lost, and rebels found it easy to make sweeping statements of condemnation. In *The American Crisis* Thomas Paine filed all Tories under "coward": "for servile, slavish, self-interested fear is the foundation of Toryism; and a man under such influence, though he may be cruel, never can be brave." Benjamin Franklin found cupidity the prime motive: "They played a deep game, staking their estates against ours." But even such a gamble was a "surer game," since the Tories had "promises to rely on" and "indemnification in cases of loss." Franklin had no objection to Tory reparations because they were "in necessity; and I think even a hired assassin has a right to his pay from his employer." Such broad categorization was remarked upon by an English observer, "for in America," he wrote, "the distinction between Whigs and Tories prevails as much at present as ever it did in England. Every man who will not drink destruction to the King, is a Tory, and liable to tar and feathers." The business of searching out and purging all Tories became so rampant that one rebel found it necessary to appeal to the better sense of his fellows:

> The observation is doubtless just, "that we should think twice before we speak once." A second thought and close examination of things and characters prevent many rash conclusions, remove ground-less prejudices, and cure a multitude of mistakes. Some, by con-stitution, believe upon the slightest evidence. . . . When here and there, and all around us, this and that man, of whom we never be-fore entertained the least suspicion, unexpectedly appears promoting the vilest cause; when our enemies prove to be in our own house-hold. . . . We are too easily led to question the veracity and integ-rity of every man. . . . A character is good until it legally and ra-tionally appears otherwise. . . . It becomes us to treat the characters of distinguished persons with candor; throw a mantle over trifling foibles; bury in a grave a little mistake; put the most favorable construction upon those instances of conduct which are not in themselves highly barefaced . . . silence the invidious and malicious; reward liberally the meritorious; and let us act throughout so that we may gain the approbation of conscience, the present age, and posterity.

The motives behind each Tory's choice of loyalty were myriad, complex, sometimes inexplicable. Aside from those truly devoted and honestly dedicated men, Tories took on many political shades. Some joined the British cause because they felt the rebels could not win. Their choice was based simply on the odds. Britain was the most powerful nation in the world, her navy the supreme com-mander of the sea. How could the rebels possibly win? "Can any of you," commented a Tory, "that think soberly upon the matter, be so deluded as to believe that Great Britain, who so lately carried her arms with success to every part of the globe . . . and whose fleets give law to the ocean, is unable to conquer us?" Alexander Graydon, a Tory himself, was in contempt of such behavior. He found Reverend Jacob Duché's chameleon nature something less than honorable. When the British took possession of Philadelphia, Reverend Duché changed his political preference from "Whig" to "Tory." Thinking "that his country was in a fair way of being subdued, he changed sides." But in his Christian way and also, pos-sibly, because any conversion to the loyalist side was an asset, Gray-don found Mr. Duché only "weak and vain, yet probably not a bad man: his habits, at least, were pious; and, with exception of this political tergiversation, his conduct exemplary."

As voluminous memorialist papers testify, the temptation of monetary gain was not often resisted. John Vardill, a professor at King's College and a minister in the Episcopal Church of New York, appeared to be honestly devoted to loyalism. He journeyed to England in 1774 and remained there throughout the war, as agent for the loyalist side. He was well paid for his activities, but in his memorial plea he requested compensation for the loss of salary, fees, and services he would have earned had he remained in America. Listing the various professional fees he had sacrificed for the cause, Vardill mentioned his "salary as assistant minister and lecturer in the church of New York £ 200 sterling, not to mention that he is next in order to the Rector, and would have succeeded (as was the established rule) on his death or removal; the salary which Government engaged to annex to his Regius Professorship £ 200 sterling." He further listed "the use of chambers, a cellar, yard and garden" which he was granted as Professor of King's College, and requested reparation for their loss as well.

It should be noted that England's generous offer to all loyalists of recompense for confiscated land and her promise of rewarding the loyalists after victory with land confiscated from the rebels induced many to join English ranks. If Great Britain lost, loyalty would be redeemed by the British Treasury; if Britain won, their fortunes would be enhanced by rebel land.

The ambition to obtain power, or the desire to preserve it, decided many votes on both sides. Officers of the Crown received their rewards from England. Their natural tendency to support the British position was further bolstered by their desire to maintain the good life. Corruption in government office had long been a complaint of colonialists, and those who lived richly through their offices would be sure to find no charity if there was a rebel victory. Royal governors, in particular, though devoted to the British constitution, did not relish their abdication from power. Viewing mankind with an acute eye, John Adams found the basic human ingredient to be vanity. Vanity, or the desire for distinction above other men, impelled man to achieve. To feel distinction and not see it in the eyes of other men is nothing. To know distinction is to have power. Some sought political control, others wished for economic rewards, and still others desired religious power.

Anglican ministers had long sought a bishopric in the North American colonies. The friction between the Anglicans and the

"Dissenters" had intensified by 1760. Anglicanism had suffered from weakness and disorganization, while the nonconformist churches had flourished and become strong under the heady freedom of America. Where the Anglicans attempted to tighten their organization, the opposition became even more adamantly opposed. The House of Representatives of Massachusetts wrote to its agent in London that "the establishment of a Protestant episcopate in America is always zealously contended for," but that such an attempt would be viewed harshly by those who "were obliged to fly their native country into a wilderness, in order peaceably to enjoy their privileges civil and religious." Religion had become tied to the issue of civil liberties. Choice of religion, as a consequence, often determined one's political preference. By 1776 most Anglican ministers in New England and the middle colonies took the loyalist side, and it appears that a majority of their congregations did likewise.

New York was the most glaring example of the religious intertwining with the political. Presbyterians, indignant that the Anglican minority, aided by the royal governors, could railroad policies through the Assembly and also deny them the right to incorporate, entered fiercely into political battle. The division of party in New York was directly centered on religious preference: William Livingston and the De Lancey factions were labelled respectively Presbyterian and Anglican; Whig or Tory was only a secondary title. The struggle over the establishment of an American episcopacy overflowed into politics, for that was the most effective area in which to achieve power. As a result, John Adams could conclude that the religious struggle was a direct cause of the American Revolution: "the apprehension of Episcopacy contributed . . . as much as any other cause, to arouse the attention not only of the inquiring mind, but of the common people, and urge them to close thinking on the constitutional authority of Parliament over the colonies."

The explanation for one man's becoming a Tory and another a rebel was complex, often ambiguous, and seldom completely visible. Some motives were plain, but each man's choice was activated by many impulses. Those in responsible positions undoubtedly believed the British constitution the best in the world, but they also were elitist in the belief that common democracy and equality were spurious and dangerous. Anglican ministers wished for ecclesiastical power but at the same time feared the loss of distinction between the elite and the common people. Royal governors might objectively believe in the rightness of the British cause, but they also dreaded the loss of their positions of prestige. Those who stood to gain economically chose for obvious reasons, but also because they believed the revolutionaries could not possibly win over such tremendous odds. Motives overlapped, and for many Tories there was as well that indefinable, never quite tangible, age-old affinity to everything British. The emotional attachment to the British flag and the long-felt kinship to the "home" country were hard ties to break. The pomp and the pageantry of royalty were infinitely more colorful than the stark new tone of common democracy. The king had long been the unifying symbol of their faith. The new ideals of the revolution had no comparable symbol. All these impulses and attachments played a part in each man's decision. If he chose openly and firmly he was branded a Tory. But there were many who never did choose. There were those who were indifferent to either cause.

Indifference, however, did not necessarily mean "neutrality." Those who sold their merchandise to the British for gold did so not because they thought Britain right and the rebels wrong, but because hard coin was preferable to continental currency. Such an act, though indifferent to the cause, placed individuals in a position dangerous to the rebel side. Indifference became a potential threat to those who were committed. Conversion became a prime objective of both factions. The Declaration of Independence was not only a philosophical justification for rebellion, but an instrument of propaganda meant to convince those Americans who had not yet chosen. There was a furious output of pamphlets and newspaper articles by Whigs and Tories, all meant as instruments of persuasion. As the confrontation became increasingly violent, more coercive measures were undertaken. If minds could not be won, force could at least compel outward obedience. Fighting against oppression and tyranny, the rebels came to suppress dissent, condone arbitrary decrees, and support strong-armed tactics. To many Americans the democratic ideals that originally prompted the conflict were lost in the fanaticism of war. No consistent policy ever was evolved to handle those who opposed the revolution. Oppression was general, but there was a wide spectrum within that oppression. There were extreme cases, such as those involving tar and feathering; but there were also others of marked leniency. Oaths of Allegiance had to be sworn, and in an age when oaths were viewed with solemn respect they were not taken lightly. The Commission for Detecting and Defeating Conspiracies in New York, especially set up to watch all suspicious acts, rarely meted out harsh punishments. Most who refused to take the Oath of Allegiance were allowed to migrate to Canada. Some were imprisoned, though rarely; and others were confined to their farms or homes. The Revolution was as much a civil war as it was a war against an external power. Americans fought Americans; the enemy was not easily discernible, and citizens viewed their neighbors without trust. Especially in civil war, intense bitterness becomes inevitable. Such bitterness was expressed in letters and pamphlets urging harsher punishment to all dissenters. Benjamin Franklin could dismiss the Tory as a "hired assassin"; George Washington could condone the execution of a Tory, regretting only that procedural rules were not carefully followed; and an unknown but vehement Whig, in a pamphlet entitled "Vengeance on the Tories!," could find them the demonic root of all evil. But the attitudes towards the loyalists and the actions upon them were usually quite different. Harsher measures might be urged but they never seemed to result in stricter enforcement. It is worthy of note that the more severe examples of punishment occurred before the declaration of war. Tar and feathering, mob actions, and the burning of houses were all pursued when the confrontation was still only verbal. In the post-revolutionary era the bitterness of the rebels was such that they could find little charity for those who had lost. But in the thick of war the rebels had no time to formulate elaborate systems of retribution.

Well into the nineteenth century the word "Tory" was reviled by an adolescent nation still suffering the pangs of growth. The need to find a common heritage in a still young history produced a stereotype of villain and hero. The American Revolution long remained a focal point, and its cast was composed of black and white players. Historians of the early period approached the Tory with little sympathy. The case was clear-cut, and George Bancroft expressed their sentiments well: "The unappeasable malice of the supporters of the ministry was bent on the most desperate and cruel efforts, while every part of the continent rung the knell of subjection. A new nation was bursting into life. . . ." But in a curious way the Tory of the 1770's was resurrected, and his belief in systematic reform, law and order, and traditional methods of operation became the "American Way." While "Tory" became a term of reproach and insult, his political creed was adopted. By the 1790's George Washington could condemn those who took part in the Whiskey Rebellion as "armed banditti"—the very term the Tories, a decade earlier, had used to describe the Continental Army and its Commander-in-Chief. Revolutionary solutions had clearly been rejected, and even Thomas Jefferson—the voice of the revolution—could claim that in America "we deal in ink only; they in blood." The American political tradition has wide boundaries indeed. It operates on the basis of pragmatic compromise that engulfs liberal and conservative positions. Any type of extremism—violence or revolution—falls without. In essence, then, the Tory standard of stable law, his emphasis upon traditional values and reform within the constitutional structure, has become the foundation of a nation once born of revolution but—almost since the day of its inception —no longer revolutionary.

# Chronology of the American Revolution

**1774**   Coercive or Intolerable Acts passed by Parliament as punitive measures against colonies (Boston Port Act; Massachusetts Government Act; Administration of Justice Act; Quartering Act).

(September 5)   First Continental Congress assembles at Philadelphia.

(October 14)   Declaration of rights and grievances adopted by Continental Congress.

(October 18)   Continental Association formed.

**1775**   (April 19)   Battles of Lexington and Concord.

(May 10)   Second Continental Congress assembles at Philadelphia.

(June 15)   George Washington appointed commander-in-chief of continental forces.

(July 6)   "Declaration of the causes and necessities of taking up arms" adopted by Continental Congress.

(November 29)   Continental Congress appoints secret committee to seek foreign aid.

(December 22)   British Parliament prohibits all trade and commerce with the thirteen colonies.

**1776**   (January)   Appearance of Thomas Paine's *Common Sense*.

(March)   Continental Congress authorizes privateering against British ships.

(May)   Continental Congress recommends that colonies suppress all vestiges of royal authority and establish popular governments.

(June 7)   Richard Henry Lee introduces resolution for independence before Continental Congress.

(July 2)   Lee's motion adopted.

(July 4)   Declaration of Independence adopted.

**1777**   Articles of Confederation adopted by Congress.

**1778**   Treaties of Commerce and Alliance between France and the United States.

11

**1780**    (September 23)   Plot of Benedict Arnold to surrender West Point to the British discovered.

**1781**    (March 1)   Articles of Confederation ratified and in effect.

(October 19)   Lord Charles Cornwallis defeated and surrenders to Americans at Yorktown.

**1783**    (September 3)   Final treaty of peace between Great Britain and United States signed at Paris.

(November 25)   Last British troops leave from New York City.

## PART ONE

# AMERICAN TORIES LOOK AT THE WORLD

*"In numbers the Tories were a very small minority"; wrote Vernon L. Parrington in* Main Currents in American Thought, *"unendowed with wealth and position they would have been negligible . . . Their most cherished dream was the institution of an American nobility, with the seal of royal favor set upon their social pretensions." Parrington admittedly wrote from a liberal-radical perspective. His essays on Thomas Paine or Thomas Jefferson bordered on the poetic. But he could scarcely appreciate, let alone understand, the Tory mentality. After all, if one believes in the sanctification of some humans, one must create devils of others. Parrington's interpretation is not only biased, but erroneous.*

*Who can tell how many Tories there were? Or how many rebels? A substantial number, some 75,000 to 100,000, left for Canada, Britain, and the West Indies during and immediately after the revolution. Several times that number remained in the states, some vigorously fighting for the crown, some quietly masking their sentiments for fear of rebel vilification and vengeance. Joseph Galloway, a Tory, claimed that four out of five Americans were, or wished to be, loyal to Britain. His estimate is too high, but so were rebel assertions of virtual colonial unanimity in the cause of independence. Certainly the Tories were not "a very small minority."*

*To be sure, many Tories were men of wealth and social position—so were many rebels—and one can readily understand why the "royal governor's set" remained loyal to the crown. But there were other causes—personal, local, special— operating to turn men to one side or the other. The subject of Tory motivations is a complex, tangled skein to be unraveled, finally, by considering the case of each individual loyalist. Taken as a group, however, "their most cherished dream" was not, as Parrington says, "the institution of an American nobility." Almost a century ago the ancestor of a Tory, Edward*

*Floyd De Lancey, tried to correct the popular image of Tories as a set of snide aristocrats interested solely in their own welfare:*

> *There can be no greater error than to suppose that the loyalists as a whole were willing to submit quietly to the exactions of the mother country, and her invasions of their rights and liberties as English subjects. As Americans they felt those grievances, and were as indignant at the treatment they were subjected to, as those of their countrymen who took up arms. But they wished to fight the battle for those rights and liberties and the redress of those grievances, with the powerful weapons which the Constitution of England gave to them as to other Englishmen— weapons which had proved successful before, as they have proved successful since, in similar emergencies . . . They desired by political agitation to force the home Government to a change of policy, or to drive it from power and place in office the foes of the oppression of the colonies. Their enemy was the ministry of Lord North, not the King of England to whom they owed, and had sworn, allegiance.*

*If some acted from selfish, narrow motives, there were countless others, conservative men of the utmost integrity, who suffered enormous personal sacrifices in behalf of their political philosophy.*

# 1

# Tory Arguments Upholding Law and Order

## LETTER FROM A VIRGINIAN, 1774[1]

That no political society can subsist unless there be an absolute supreme power lodged somewhere in the society, has been universally held as an uncontrollable maxim in theory by all writers on government, from Aristotle down to Sidney and Locke, and has been

[1] *Letter from a VIRGINIAN to the Members of the Congress to be held at Philadelphia, on the first of September, 1774* (New York, 1774), pp. 11, 13, 24–25.

as universally adopted in practice. . . . As long as government subsists, subjects owe an implicit obedience to the laws of the supreme power, from which there can be no appeal but to Heaven. We for some years past have been multiplying ineffectual resolves, petitions and remonstrances, and advancing claims of rights, etc. Our Petitions have at last been neglected, or rejected, or censured; the principles on which we found our claims have been formally denied. To what, or to whom, shall we have recourse? Shall we appeal to the King of Massachusetts Bay, to the King of Connecticut, to the King of Rhode Island, against the King of Great Britain, to rescind the acts of Parliament of Great Britain, to dispense with the Laws, to which as a necessary and efficient part of that body, he has recently given his assent? The Colonies are constitutionally independent of each other; they formally acknowledge themselves loyal and dutiful subjects of his Majesty George III. But several claim an exemption from the authority of the British Parliament. . . .

What part then, Gentlemen, have you left to act, but to propose . . . some practical plan of accommodation, and to obey? Shall the time of so respectable an assembly be squandered, in advancing the claims of right, that have been urged and rejected a thousand times; that have been heard, considered, solemnly debated, and decided by the only power on earth who has a right to decide them? Shall the opinions and desires of a small part of the community prevail against the opinions and desires of the Majority of the community? What new species of eloquence can be invented to persuade? What new logic to convince the understandings of our fellow subjects? Shall the British senate be governed by the pernicious maxims of a Polish Diet, and the veto of a single member, or a few members, however distinguished by extraordinary wisdom, and virtue, obstruct or suspend or annul the legislation of a great Nation?

On the subject of taxation, the authority of Mr. Locke is generally quoted . . . as paramount to all other authority whatever. His treatise on government, as far as his ideas are practicable, with the corrupt materials of all governments, is undoubtedly a most beautiful theory. . . . Let us respect it as the opinions of a wise, and virtuous philosopher and patriot, but let us likewise, as good subjects, revere the laws of the land, the collected wisdom of ages, and make them the rule of our political conduct. Let not Mr. Locke be quoted partially, by those who have read him, to mislead thousands who never read him. When he is brought as an authority, that no subject can be justly taxed without his consent; why don't they add his own explanation of that consent? i.e. "The consent of the majority, giving it either by themselves, or their representatives chosen by them." Do we compose the majority of the British community? Are we, or are we not, of that community? If we are of that community, but are not represented, are we not in the same situation with the numerous body of copyholders, with the inhabitants of many wealthy and populous towns, in short, with a very great number of our fellow subjects, who have no votes in elections? Shall we affirm that these are so; and at the same time, be too proud to solicit a representation? . . . Shall we plunge at once into anarchy, and reject all accommodation with a government because there are imperfections in it, as there are in all things, and in all men?

### SAMUEL SEABURY'S ADDRESS, 1774 [2]

I shall make no apology for addressing myself to you, the Merchants of the city of New York, upon the present unhappy and distressed state of our country. My subject will necessarily lead me to make some remarks on your past and present conduct, in this unnatural contention between our parent country and us. I am duly sensible of what importance you are to the community, and of the weight and influence you must have in the conduct of all our public affairs. I know that the characters of many of you are truly respectable and I shall endeavor to express what I have to say to you, consistently, with that decency and good manner which are due, not only to you, but to all mankind. . . .

Nor, upon the other hand, ought you to be displeased with the man who shall point out your errors; supposing you have acted wrong. To err is common,—I wish it was uncommon to persist in error. But such is the pride of the human heart, that when we have once taken a wrong step, we think it an impeachment of our wisdom and prudence to retreat. A kind of sullen, sulky obstinacy takes possession of us; and though, in the hour of calm reflection our hearts should condemn us, we had rather run the risk of being condemned by the world too, than own the possibility of our having been mistaken. . . .

Look at the Suffolk Resolves, from Massachusetts, which they adopted, "approved and recommended." Look into their addresses to the people of Great Britain, to the inhabitants of the colonies in

[2] Samuel Seabury, *The Congress Canvassed: or, An Examination into the Conduct of the Delegates, etc. Addressed to the Merchants of New York* (New York, 1774), pp. 3–5, 10–11.

general, and to those of Quebec in particular. They all tend, under cover of strong and lamentable cries about liberty, and the rights of Englishmen, to degrade and contravene the authority of the British parliament over the British dominions; on which authority the rights of Englishmen are, in a great measure, founded; and on the due support of which authority, the liberty and property of the inhabitants, even of this country, must ultimately depend. They all tend to raise jealousies, to excite animosities, to ferment discords between us and our mother country. Not a word of peace and reconciliation—not even a soothing expression. No concessions are offered on our part, nor even a possibility of their treating with us left. The parliament must give up their whole authority—repeal all the acts, in a lump, which the Continental Congress have found fault with, and trust, for the future, to our honor to pay them just so much submission as we shall think convenient. . . .

Consider now, and tell me, what right or power has any assembly on the continent to appoint delegates, to represent their province in such a congress as that which lately met at Philadelphia? The assemblies have but a delegated authority themselves. They are but the representatives of the people; they cannot therefore have even the shadow of right, to delegate that authority to three or four persons, even should these persons be of their own number, which were delegated by the people to their whole body conjunctively. Delegates, so appointed, are, at best, but delegates of delegates, but representatives of representatives. . . .

The people are not bound by any act of their representatives, till it hath received the approbation of the other branches of the legislature. No delegates, therefore, can in any *true* sense be called the *representation* of a province, unless they be appointed by the joint act of the whole legislature of the province. When, therefore, the delegates at Philadelphia, in the preamble to their Bill of Rights, and in their letter to his Excellency General Gage, styled their body "a full and free representation of . . . all the colonies from Nova Scotia to Georgia," they were guilty of a piece of impudence which was never equalled since the world began. . . .

The legislative authority of any province cannot extend farther than the province extends. None of its acts are binding an inch beyond its limits. How then can it give authority to a few persons to meet other persons, from other provinces, to make rules and laws for the whole continent? In such a case, the Carolinas, Virginia, Maryland, and the four New England colonies, might make laws to bind Philadelphia, New Jersey and New York; that is—they might make laws whose operation should extend farther than the authority by which they were enacted, extended. Before such a mode of legislation can take place, the constitution of our colonies must be subverted, and their present independency on each other must be annihilated. And after it was accomplished, we should be in a situation a thousand times worse, than our present dependence on Great Britain, should all the difficulties we complain of be real, and all the grievances some people affect to fear, fall upon us.

### JABEZ FISHER OF PENNSYLVANIA, 1774 [3]

The Americans have now acquired a considerable share of property, though it must be confessed, by no means so much as the folly and extravagance of a few have taught our superiors to believe. In proportion to this property, the most plain and evident principle of justice, pronounces the equity of their being taxed in order to defray the expense which their own safety requires. If more than the colonies can bear is necessary, their mother country holds herself ready, to lend her assistance, to secure them from foreign invasion, oppression and misery. This she ever has done, and as long as she is actuated by the principles of sound policy, she will and must continue to do so.

The power of making war, of protecting and defending British subjects, in every part of the world, and of forming, directing, and *executing that protection,* is constitutionally vested in the crown alone. The subject has a right to demand it whenever he is in danger. This right is purchased by his allegiance, which is the reciprocal consideration duly paid for it. America, consisting of a number of colonies in their infant state, and independent of each other, is in a particular manner dependent on this power and has a right to demand an exertion of it to insure its safety. And accordingly, during the late war, she received the full advantages of it, without which, in her disunited state, she, in all probability, must have fallen before the most cruel and barbarous of all countries. The preservation of America is of the utmost importance to Great Britain. A loss of it to the British crown would greatly diminish its strength, and the possession of it to another nation, would give an increase of wealth and power, totally inconsistent with the safety of Britons. *If* then the power of protection is rightfully and solely

[3] A Pennsylvanian [Jabez Fisher], *Americus and his Principles compared with those of the Approved Advocates for America* (Philadelphia, 1774), pp. 7–11, 15–16.

ested in the crown; *if* America is of so much importance to her
nother country; and *if* it is just and reasonable that she should con-
ribute towards her own defense, so essential to her own and the
happiness of Great Britain; *will any be so absurd as to deny the
reasonableness, the necessity, of the crown's having some certainty
that she will pay her proportion of aids when requisite and demanded?*

If then it is reasonable that America should be taxed, towards
her own safety, and her safety depends on her enabling the crown
to secure it; *if* without this, she may be lost to her mother country
and deprived of her civil as well as religious rights; *if she has been
thus negligent of her duty, and perversely obstinate,* when those
rights and her own preservation required a contrary behavior; *if
she* has, notwithstanding, been preserved, in a great measure at
the expense of her mother country, and if, *under her present circumstances and disunion, it appears from experience,* that *the
crown can have no dependence,* that she will act differently on future occasions, does it not then become the *indispensable* duty of a
British parliament to interfere, and compel her to do what is so
reasonable and necessary for her preservation! Shall the colonies
be lost to the British dominions through their own obstinacy, caprice and folly; and shall not Great Britain whose interest is in-
separably united with theirs, endeavor to prevent it? Shall she stand
by, an inactive spectator, indifferent to her own and their welfare,
and not make the *least essay* towards avoiding the consequential
mischiefs?

## A TORY PASQUINADE OF THE NEW YORK REBELS, 1774 [4]

At a meeting of the TRUE Sons of Liberty, in the City of New
York, July 27, 1774, properly convened;

*Present:* John Calvin, John Knox, Roger Rumpus, etc.

1. Resolved, That in this general Time of resolving, we have as
good a right to resolve as the most resolute.
2. Resolved, That we have the whole Sense of the City, County,
Province, and all the Colonies, concentrated in our own Persons.
3. Resolved, *Therefore,* that *a general* Congress (saving *Appear-
ances*) would be unnecessary and useless.
4. Resolved, That the Distresses of our Brethren —— in —— the

[4] Edward Floyd De Lancey, ed., *History of New York during the Revolutionary War . . . by Thomas Jones* (New York, 1879), vol. 1, pp. 465–66.

—— Lord, of Boston, are unprecedented, illegal, [and diab]olica
the People of *Massachusetts Bay* being thereby required to mal
Reparation for Damages [and tres]passes by them done and con
mitted, *only* in Support of their own *proper* and *avowed* Purpos
to [establish] one GRAND REPUBLIC throughout this ill-go
erned CONTINENT: of which, and for the sole [use] and Benel
of the whole, the MASSACHUSITES *only* propose themselves as tl
Heads and Directors; in [order that] the said Continent, for the f
ture, may be more justly and equitably ruled, directed, and *pr*
*tected.*

5. Resolved, *Therefore,* that WE will concur with them in ever
measure for effectuating the [said] salutary purpose; being con
vinced, as were *their* and *our* Forefathers, that this is the only [wa
whereby an effectual stop may be put to the alarming growth 
PRELACY, QUAKERISM, and LIBERTY OF CONSCIENCE: 
all of which, by the most obliging Methods of prosecuting, persecu
ting, [and] hanging, or drowning, both *they* and *we* have ever bee
sworn Enemies; so will continue, *till the End of Time*—be it eve
so endless.

6. Resolved, That the *fittest* Persons to carry on this great, good
necessary and godly Work, are [those whom] the Freeholders, i
their respective Counties and Colonies, have elected to be thei
Representatives. [They are] *supposed* to be Men of Conscience an
Understanding—but such only as OURSELVES; who have [n
claim] to Speculation and Refinement; but simply fitted, by ou
lives and Conversation, for *right*[ful doings]; which are the onl
Doings, in these distressful times, that ought to go right forwar

7. Resolved, with our brethren of this city, that these Resolve
and any we may *afterwards* see [fit] to promulgate, shall be ap
proved by all *sensible* and *good* men in our parent country; an
that [they shall] even make that ungracious varlet LORD NORTI
*shake in his shoes,* (when he *sees* them) and [split] his breeches.

8. Resolved, with our brethren of South Carolina, that we wil
pay the expence of *printing* these [resolves].

9. Resolved, according to the *third* resolve of our brethren o
*New Brunswick* that any Act or [acts] of Parliament which preven
the colonies from triumphing over the liberties, sporting with th
[goods] or at will claiming the properties of the Ministry, is a crue
oppression in which all the Colonies [are] intimately concerned.

10. Resolved, with our brethren of *Annapolis* that the non-pay
ment of debt contracted with [England] is the only way to save th

credit of those, who have got no money to pay their debts *with*.

11. Resolved, that a *strict adherence* to a non-importation and non-exportation agreement, which was so easily effected, and so *faithfully observed,* in the time of the *Stamp Act,* is the only *certain* [way] of coming at the *naked* truth; without which we shall never be able to unveil the covert, and close, [and wicked] designs of the d——d Ministry, to ruin us.

12. Resolved, that because *Boston* is *undeservedly* chastised, all the other colonies ought to be deservedly.

13. Resolved, that it is a *general* mark of patriotism, to eat the King's bread, and abuse him for [it].

14. Resolved, that the best way of approving our loyalty, is to spit in the said King's face; as the means of *opening* his *eyes.*

15. Resolved, lastly, that every man, woman, or child, who doth not agree with our sentiments, whether he, she, or they, understand them or not, is an enemy to his country, wheresoever he was born, and a Jacobite in principle, whatever he may think of it; and that he ought at least to be tarred and feathered, if not hanged, drawn and quartered; all statutes, laws, and ordinances whatsoever to the contrary notwithstanding.

> By Order of the Meeting,
> *Ebenezer Snuffle,* Secretary

## WILLIAM EDDIS OF MARYLAND, 1775 [5]

The present unhappy contention between the mother country and her colonies is a matter of the deepest concern to every honest, every feeling mind; it is, therefore, the indispensable duty of every friend of society, to study and to pursue those methods, which may lead to a perfect reconciliation, and the establishment of a permanent union between Great Britain and America.

The principle of parliamentary taxation over this extensive part of the empire, is generally denied by all ranks, and denominations of men; the grand subject of controversy, therefore, that prevails at present, respects the most eligible method to obtain redress. On this point, there appears a division of sentiment, which has given rise to heart-burnings and discontent; and, in some degree, struck at the root of that harmony which, at this important period, ought to guide and influence every action.

[5] Letter of William Eddis, *Maryland Gazette,* February 14, 1775.

In opposition to measures dictated by calmness and moderation (a steady adherence to which, it was generally supposed, would be attended with the most happy effects), a military appearance is assumed—subscriptions are industriously making for the purchase of arms, ammunition, etc. and the severest censure is indiscriminately passed on those persons who happen to dissent from the popular opinion, and prefer more conciliating methods of accommodation.

It is certain that there are many in this, and other provinces, who object to the spirit of violence, which seems at this time to predominate. Convinced of the propriety of their sentiments, and in the integrity of their hearts, they conceive the cause of America may be totally injured by a precipitate, and unnecessary defiance of the power of Great Britain; they firmly believe, that a respectful behavior to their sovereign and their mother country—a dutiful and constitutional application to the throne—and a firm perseverance in virtuous, though pacific principles, will, in the issue, be productive of the most felicitous consequences. Actuated by such considerations, they cannot be reconciled to those violent extremes which have been too rashly adopted by many; and which they are anxious to establish, as the only feasible plan of terminating the present dissensions.

On deliberate reflection, it can hardly be imagined, that the mother country has formed the least intention of reducing these provinces to a state of abject servility, by the force of arms; the natural connection—the close ties—and nice dependencies, which exist between the different parts of the empire, forbid indulging any conclusions of so melancholy a nature. She will be more just—more tender to her offspring—the voice of reason will prevail—our grievances will be redressed—and she will be found, to the end of time, a kind—a fostering parent! But admitting that Great Britain were determined to enforce a submission to all her mandates; even in that case, we have little cause to apprehend that she will unsheath the sword, and establish her decrees in the blood of thousands. A more safe and certain method is obvious; a small proportion of her naval power would entirely shut up our harbors—suspend trade—impoverish the inhabitants—promote intestine divisions—and involve us in all the horrors of anarchy and confusion. To avoid evils, even great as these, we are not meanly to bend the neck, and submit to every innovation. But when there is no prospect of such calamities, why are we to form ideas of battles and of slaughter? Why are our coasts to resound with hostile preparations? The demon of discord to stalk at large? And friends and kindred forget the peaceful bonds of amity and love?

## GOVERNOR WILLIAM FRANKLIN'S LETTER
## TO THE NEW JERSEY LEGISLATURE, 1776 [6]

Let me exhort you to avoid, above all things, the traps of Independency and Republicanism now set for you, however temptingly they may be baited. Depend upon it, you can never place yourselves in a happier situation than in your ancient constitutional dependency on Great-Britain. No independent state ever was or ever can be so happy as we have been, and might still be, under that government. I have early and often warned you of the pernicious designs of many pretended patriots; who, under the mask of zeal for reconciliation, have been from the first insidiously promoting a system of measures, purposely calculated for widening the breach between the two countries, so far as to let in an Independent Republican Tyranny—the worst and most debasing of all possible tyrannies. They well know that this has not even a chance of being accomplished, but at the expence of the lives and properties of many thousands of the honest people of this country—yet *these*, it seems, are as nothing in the eyes of such desperate gamesters! But remember, Gentlemen, that I now tell you, that should they (contrary to all probability) accomplish their baneful purpose, yet their government will not be lasting. It will never suit a people who have once tasted the sweets of British liberty under a British constitution. When the present high fever shall abate of its warmth, and the people are once more able coolly to survey and compare their past with their then situation, they will, as naturally as the sparks fly upwards, wreak their vengeance on the heads of those who, taking advantage of their delirium, had plunged them into such difficulties and distress.

This, Gentlemen, I well know, is not language to the times. But it is better, it is honest truth flowing from a heart that is ready to shed its best blood for this country. A real patriot can seldom or ever speak popular language. A false one will never suffer himself to speak anything else. The last will often be popular because he will always conform himself to the present humor and passions of the people, that he may the better gratify his private ambition,

[6] Frederick W. Ricord and William Nelson, eds., *Documents Relating to the Colonial History of the State of New Jersey* (Newark, New Jersey, 1886), vol. 10, pp. 726–28.

and promote his own sinister designs. The first will most generally
be unpopular, because his conscience will not permit him to be
guilty of such base compliances, and because he will even serve
the people, if in his power, against their own inclinations, though
he be sure that he thereby risks his ruin or destruction. I am not
insensible of the dangers I am likely to incur, but I do not regard
them. It is the part of an ignoble mind to decline doing good for
fear of evil that might follow. I bear no enmity to any man who
means well, however we may differ in political sentiments. I most
heartily wish you, Gentlemen, and the people of this once happy
province may again enjoy peace and prosperity, and I shall ever
particularly honor and esteem such of you and them as have dared,
with an honest and manly firmness, in these worst of times, to avow
their loyalty to the best of sovereigns, and manifest their attachment to their legal Constitution. As to my own part, I have no
scruple to repeat at this time what I formerly declared to the Assembly—*That no Office or Honor in the Power of the Crown to bestow,
will ever influence me to forget or neglect the Duty I owe my Country, nor the most furious Rage of the most intemperate Zealots
induce me to swerve from the Duty I owe His Majesty.*

### PETER OLIVER'S ACCOUNT, 1776 [7]

The revolt of *North America,* from their Allegiance to and
Connection with the Parent State, seems to be as striking a phe-
nomenon, in the political world, as hath appeared for many ages
past; and perhaps it is a singular one. For, by adverting to the his-
toric page, we shall find no revolt of colonies, whether under the
Roman or any other state, but what originated from severe oppressions, derived from the supreme head of the state, or from those
whom he had entrusted as his substitutes to be governors of his
provinces. In such cases, the elasticity of human nature has been ex-
erted, to throw off the burdens which the subjects have groaned
under; and in most of the instances which are recorded in history,
human nature will still justify those efforts.

But for a colony, which had been nursed, in its infancy, with
the most tender care and attention; which had been indulged with
every gratification that the most forward child could wish for;

[7] Douglass Adair and John A. Schutz, eds., *Peter Oliver's Origin and Progress
of the American Rebellion: A Tory View* (Stanford: Stanford University Press,
1961), p. 3. Reprinted with the permission of the Henry E. Huntington Library
and Art Gallery, San Marino, California.

which had even bestowed upon it such liberality, which its infancy and youth could not *think* to ask for; which had been repeatedly saved from impending destruction, sometimes by an aid unsought —at other times by assistance granted to them from their own repeated humble supplications; for such colonies to plunge into an unnatural rebellion, and in the reign of a sovereign, too, whose public virtues had distinguished him as an ornament of the human species—this surely, to an attentive mind, must strike with some degree of astonishment; and such a mind would anxiously wish for a veil to throw over the nakedness of human nature.

### REVEREND CHARLES INGLIS, 1777 [8]

Never, I will boldly and without hesitation pronounce it, never was a more just, more honorable, or necessary cause for taking up arms than that which now calls you into the field. It is the cause of truth against falsehood, of loyalty against rebellion, of legal government against usurpation, of Constitutional Freedom against Tyranny—in short it is the cause of human happiness of millions against outrage and oppression. Your generous efforts are required to assert the rights of your amiable, injured sovereign—they are required to restore your civil constitution which was formed by the wisdom of the ages, and was the admiration and envy of mankind— under which we and our ancestors enjoy liberty, happiness and security—but is now subverted to make room for a motley fabric, that is perfectly adapted to popular tyranny. Your bleeding country, through which destitution and ruin are driving in full career, from which peace, order, commerce, and useful industry are banished—your loyal friends and relations groaning in bondage under the iron scourge of persecution and oppression—all these now call upon you for succor and redress.

It is not wild, insatiable ambition which sports with lives and fortunes of mankind that leads you forth, driven from your peaceful habitations for no other cause than honoring your King, as God has commanded; you have taken up the sword to vindicate his just authority, to support your excellent constitution, to defend your families, your liberty, and property, to secure to yourselves and your posterity that inheritance of constitutional freedom to which you were born; and all this against the violence of usurped power, which

[8] John Wolfe Lydekker, *The Life and Letters of Charles Inglis* (London: The Society for Promoting Christian Knowledge, 1936), p. 257. Reprinted with the permission of the publisher.

would deny you even the right of judgment or of choice, which would rend from you the protection of your parent state, and eventually place you—astonishing infatuation and madness—place you under the despotic rule of our inveterate Popish enemies, the inveterate enemies of our religion, our country and liberties.

# 2
# Tory Experiences in Revolutionary America

## LETTER OF REVEREND SAMUEL PETERS, HAVING FLED FROM CONNECTICUT TO BOSTON, 1774 [1]

REVEREND SIR: The riots and mobs that have attended me and my house, set on by the Governor of *Connecticut,* have compelled me to take up my abode here; and the clergy of *Connecticut* must fall a sacrifice, with the several churches, very soon to the rage of the puritan nobility, if the old serpent, that dragon, is not bound. . . .

Spiritual iniquity rides in high places, with halberts, pistols, and swords. See the Proclamation I send you by my nephew, and their pious Sabbath day, the 4th of last month, when the preachers and magistrats left the pulpits, etc., for the gun and drum, and set off for *Boston,* cursing the King and Lord *North,* General *Gage,* of *England.* And for my telling the church people not to take up arms, etc., it being high treason, etc., the Sons of Liberty have almost killed one of my church, tarred and feathered two, abused others; and on the sixth day destroyed my windows, and rent my clothes, even my gown, etc., crying out, down with the church, the rags of Popery; their rebellion is obvious; treason is common and robbery is their daily diversion; the *Lord* deliver us from anarchy.

## LETTER OF ANN HULTON FROM BOSTON, 1774 [2]

The most shocking cruelty was exercised a few nights ago, upon a poor old man, a tidesman, one Malcolm. . . . A quarrel

[1] Peter Force, ed., *American Archives* (Washington, D.C., 1837–1853), Series IV: vol. 1, pp. 716–17.
[2] Ann Hulton, *Letters of a Loyalist Lady,* with an Introduction by Harold Murdock (Cambridge: Harvard University Press, 1927), pp. 70–71. Reprinted with the permission of the publisher.

27

was picked with him. He was afterward taken, and tarred and feathered. There's no law that knows a punishment for the greatest crimes beyond what this is, of cruel torture. And this instance exceeds any other before it. He was stripped stark naked, one of the severest cold nights this winter, his body covered all over with tar, then with feathers, his arm dislocated in tearing off his clothes. He was dragged in a cart, with thousands attending, some beating him with clubs and knocking him out of the cart, then in again. They gave him several severe whippings, at different parts of the town. This spectacle of horror and sportive cruelty was exhibited for about five hours.

The unhappy wretch they say behaved with the greatest intrepidity and fortitude. All the while before he was taken, he defended himself a long time against numbers; and afterwards, when under torture they demanded of him to curse his masters, the king, governors, etc. which they could not make him do, but he still cried, Curse all Traitors. They brought him to the gallows and put a rope about his neck saying they would hang him; he said he wished they would, but that they could not for God was above the Devil. The doctors say that it is impossible that this poor creature can live. They say his flesh comes off his back in stakes.

It is the second time he has been tarred and feathered and this is looked upon more to intimidate the judges and others than a spite to the unhappy victim, though they owe him a grudge for some things, particularly, he was with Governor Tryon in the Battle with the Regulators. . . . The Governor has declared that he was of great service to him in that affair, by his undaunted spirit encountering the greatest dangers.

Governor Tryon had sent him a gift of ten guineas just before this inhuman treatment. He has a wife and family and an aged father and mother who, they say, saw the spectacle which no indifferent person can mention without horror.

These few instances among many serve to show the abject state of government and the licentiousness and barbarism of the times. There's no magistrate that dare or will act to suppress the outrages. No person is secure. There are many objects pointed at, at this time, and when once marked out for vengeance, their ruin is certain.

## INTIMIDATING AN OLD TORY, 1775 [3]

This morning Mr. John Case, an old man of near sixty years of age, from Long Island, was entreated by an acquaintance of his to go to the house of Jasper Drake, tavern-keeper . . . where he was told Captain McD——l, Captain S——s, and others wanted to converse with him on politics. He went, and soon entered into conversation with Captain McD——l, who attempted to convince him that he was in an error, but not being able to effect it, politely left him. Captain S——s, with several other persons, then attacked him with the force of their eloquence and noise, but Case said he was an unlearned man, and but of few words—that he could not reply to above one. That he judged, however, the fairest way to come at the truth would be to recur to the origin of the present contest between Great Britain and the Colonies, and to trace from the time of the stamp act, the encroachments of ministerial power, and the increasing demands for provincial privileges. This was objected to by Captain S——s, as it would require too much time and attention to discuss. He said that he would question him a little, and asked Case whether the king had not violated his coronation oath? Mr. Case replied, that he thought he had not, and reasoned on this and other matters in as cool a manner as possible, in order not to irritate Captain S——s, who, however, soon grew warm, and branded Case with the appellation of Tory, and told him that if he was in Connecticut . . . he would be put to death. S——s then demanded of Case whether, if the Bostonians were to take up arms, he would fight for the king? Case answered, that if he fought on either side, he would certainly fight for no one else, as he conceived King George to be his lawful sovereign, for the minister a few days before prayed for our rightful sovereign Lord King George the Third, on which S——s replied he was sorry that he had turned churchman, where such prayers were used; Case replied, these expressions were delivered the preceding Sunday by Dr. Rodgers at the Presbyterian meeting, for he himself was a Presbyterian. After a few more queries and replies of a similar nature, S——s told him that he would not suffer a Tory to sit in company with gentlemen, placed a chair in the chimney corner, caught Case by the arm, and forced him into it. He then called for a negro boy, who belonged to the house, and ordered him to sit along with him; for that he (Case) was only fit

[3] Frank Moore, ed., *Diary of the American Revolution* (New York, 1858), pp. 9–10.

to sit in company with slaves; but the negro had too much understanding to reply. Mr. Case then called for some wine, and offered
it to the company, but S——s refused to accept it, pushed him down
in the chair where he had before placed him, and ordered the rest
not to drink with a Tory; and further, that whoever spoke to Case,
should forfeit a bowl of toddy, which was exacted by him from two
persons who happened to disobey his mandates. S——s then told
Case that his age protected him, for if he was a young man, he
would have placed him on a red-hot gridiron; and after he had
detained this old man as long as he thought proper, he dismissed
him.

### THE PROSELYTIZATION OF A RHODE ISLAND TORY, 1775 [4]

In the Upper House
Providence, April 25, 1775

We, the subscribers, professing true allegiance to His Majesty
King George the Third, beg leave to dissent from the vote of the
House of Magistrates, for enlisting, raising and embodying an army
of observation, of fifteen hundred men, to repel any insult or violence that may be offered to the inhabitants; and also, if it be necessary for the safety and preservation of any of the colonies, to march
them out of this colony, to join and co-operate with the forces of
the neighboring colonies.

Because we are of opinion that such a measure will be attended
with the most fatal consequences to our charter privileges; involve
the country in all the horrors of a civil war; and, as we conceive, is
an open violation of the oath of allegiance which we have severally
taken, upon our admission into the respective offices we now hold
in the colony.

*Joseph Wanton*  *Thomas Wickes*
*Darius Sessions*  *William Potter*

To the Honorable General Assembly of the colony of Rhode Island, to be holden at Providence, the 31st day of October, A.D.
1775: The Memorial of Darius Sessions, of said Providence, humbly
showeth: That at a session of the General Assembly, in April last,
an act passed for raising and embodying fifteen hundred men, for
the defence of the colony, etc.; against which, your memorialist en-

[4] John R. Bartlett, ed., *Records of the Colony of Rhode Island* (Providence,
Rhode Island, 1862), vol. 7, pp. 311, 398–99.

tered a protest, expressed in terms which greatly displeased the General Assembly and the good people of the colony, for which he is very sorry, and now craves their forgiveness; and as he is in principle a friend to the liberties of America, it is his determination to unite and co-operate with his countrymen in defending all our invaluable rights and privileges.

### DANIEL COXE TO CORTLAND SKINNER, ATTORNEY GENERAL OF NEW JERSEY, 1775 [5]

Such is the present infatuated temper of the times, and the minds of men daily increasing in madness and phrensy, that they are ready to enter upon the most daring and desperate attempts. A prostration of law and government naturally opens the door for the licentious and abandoned to exercise every malevolent inclination—what then have men of property not to fear and apprehend, and particularly those who happen and are known to differ in sentiment from the generality? They become a mark at once for popular fury, and those who are esteemed friends to government devoted for destruction. They are not even allowed to preserve a neutrality, and passiveness becomes a crime. Those who are not for us are against us, is the cry, and public necessity calls for and will justify their destruction, both life and property. In short, those deemed Tories have everything to fear from the political persecuting spirit now prevailing. The Lex Talionis is talked of should General Gage exercise any severity on those prisoners lately taken in forcing the entrenchments on Bunker's Hill and every man who may be deemed disaffected to the present measures of America must make atonement for their sufferings. This I can assure you is mentioned as a matter determined upon, and I doubt not in the least of its being put in execution should the General proceed against those unhappy people as is expected he will, in Terrorem.

### ACCOUNT OF THE REV. JONATHAN BOUCHER, 1775 [6]

The principles and ways of thinking of Whigs and Tories, or of Republicans and Loyalists, are hardly more different than are

[5] Frederick W. Ricord and William Nelson, eds., *Documents Relating to the Colonial History of the State of New Jersey* (Newark, New Jersey, 1886), vol. 10, p. 654.

[6] Jonathan Boucher, *Reminiscences of an American Loyalist* (New York: Houghton Mifflin Company, 1925), pp. 118–24.

their tempers. The latter have a foolish good-nature and improvidence about them which leads them often to hurt their own interests by promoting those of their adversaries, when the objects for which they contended are removed; but the former never forgives, never ceases to effect his purposes of being revenged on those he has once called his enemies. Mr. Sprigg was a thorough Whig, and I perhaps as thorough a Loyalist; as appeared on the least fracas of the kind in which I was involved, and which now soon took place. . . .

A public fast was ordained. In America, as in the Grand Rebellion in England, much execution was done by sermons. Those persons who have read any out of the great number of Puritan sermons that were then printed as well as preached, will cease to wonder that so many people were worked up into such a state of frenzy; and I who either heard, or heard of, many similiar discourses from the pulpits in America, felt the effects of them no less than they had before been felt here. My curate was but a weak brother, yet a strong Republican, i.e., as far as he knew how. The sermon he had preached on a former fast, though very silly, was still more exceptionable as contributing to blow the coals of sedition. Its silliness perhaps made it even more mischievous; for to be very popular, it is, I believe, necessary to be very like the bulk of the people, that is, wrongheaded, ignorant, and prone to resist authority. And I am persuaded, whenever it happens that a really sensible man becomes the idol of the people, it must be owing to his possessing a talent of letting himself down to their level. It remains to be proved, however, that ever a really sensible person did take this part; I think the contrary may be proved. As, however, Mr. Harrison's practice as well as preaching were now beginning to be exceptionable, that is, by his setting about and promoting factious associations and subscriptions, it was thought necessary that on the approaching fast-day, which was a day of great expectation, I should make a point of appearing in my own pulpit. . . .

When the fast-day came I set off, accompanied by Mr. Walter Dulany, since made a major in a Provincial Loyal Regiment, and was at my church at least a quarter of an hour before the usual time of beginning service. But behold, Mr. Harrison was in the desk, and was expected also, as I was soon told, to preach. This was not agreeable: but of how little significance was this compared to what I next saw, viz. my church filled with not less than 200 armed men, under the command of Mr. Osborne Sprigg, who soon let me know

I was not to preach. I returned for answer that the pulpit was my own, and as such I would use it; and that there was but one way by which they could keep me out of it, and that was by taking away my life. In church I managed to place myself so as to have the command of the pulpit, and told my curate at his peril not to attempt to dispossess me. Sundry messages were sent, and applications made to me, to relinquish my purpose; but as I knew it was my duty, and thought also that it was my interest, not to relinquish it, I persisted. And so at the proper time, with my sermon in one hand and a loaded pistol in the other, like Nehemiah, I prepared to ascend the steps of the pulpit, when behold, one of my friends (Mr. David Crawford of Upper Marlborough) having got behind me, threw his arms around mine and held me fast. He assured me on his honor he had both seen and heard the most positive orders given to twenty men picked out for the purpose to fire on me the moment I got into the pulpit, which therefore he never would permit me to do, unless I was stronger than he and two or three others who stood close to him. I entreated him and them to go with me into the pulpit, as my life seemed to myself to depend on my not suffering these outrageous people to carry their point; and I suppose we should all be safe while we were all together, for Mr. Crawford and those with him were rather against than for me in politics. In all these cases I argued that once to flinch was forever to invite danger; and that as I could never be out of the reach of such men till I was out of the country, my only policy was, if possible, to intimidate them, as in some degree I had hitherto done. My well-wishers however prevailed—by force rather than by persuasion; and when I was down it is horrid to recollect what a scene of confusion ensued. A large party insisted I was right in claiming and using my own pulpit; but Sprigg and his company were now grown more violent, and soon managed so as to surround me, and to exclude every moderate man. Seeing myself thus circumstanced, it occurred to me that things seemed now indeed to be growing alarming, and that there was but one way to save my life. This was by seizing Sprigg, as I immediately did, by the collar, and with my cocked pistol in the other hand, assuring him that if any violence was offered to me I would instantly blow his brains out, as I most certainly would have done. I then told him that if he pleased he might conduct me to my horse, and I would leave them. This he did, and we marched together upwards of a hundred yards, I with one hand fastened in his collar and a pistol in the other, guarded by his whole company, whom he had the meanness to order to play on their drums the Rogues' March all the way we went, which they did. All farther that I could then do was to declare, as loud as I could speak, that he had now proved himself to be a complete coward and scoundrel.

Thus ended this dreadful day, which was a Thursday. On the Sunday following I again went to the same church, was again opposed, though more feebly than before, owing to an idea that I never would think of making another attempt. I preached the same sermon I should have preached on the Thursday, with some comments on the transactions of that day. After sermon, notice having been spread of my being at Church, a larger body assembled, and I found myself again surrounded and hustled. But placing my back against a pillar of the church, and being a little raised, I again began to bawl and to harangue, and again got off; so that this affray ended in a war of words.

These attacks, however, now became so frequent and so furious, and the time, moreover, was coming on fast when if I did not associate, and take the oaths against legal government, I should certainly be proscribed, and, what seemed still worse, not have it in my power to get out of their clutches; for on the 10th of September all farther intercourse with Great Britain was to be stopped; so that I now began to have serious thoughts of making my retreat to England. It was far too plain that such a step could not but be in a manner ruinous to all my interests in America, which were then all the interests I had in the world; but it was alas! still plainer that to stay would too probably be equally fatal to my property and my life. . . .

## SAMUEL CURWEN OF SALEM FLEES TO PHILADELPHIA, 1775 [7]

Since the late unhappy affairs at Concord and Lexington, finding the spirit of the people to rise on every fresh alarm (which has been almost hourly) and their tempers to get more and more soured and malevolent against all moderate men, whom they see fit to reproach as enemies of their country by the name of Tories, among whom I am unhappily (though unjustly) ranked, and unable longer to bear their undeserved reproaches and menaces hourly denounced against myself and others, I think it a duty I owe

[7] George Atkinson Ward, ed., *Journal and Letters of the Late Samuel Curwen* (New York, 1842), pp. 25–29.

myself to withdraw for a while from the storm which to my foreboding mind is approaching. Having in vain endeavored to persuade my wife to accompany me, her apprehensions of danger from an incensed soldiery, a people licentious and enthusiastically mad and broken loose from all the restraints of law or religion being less terrible to her than a short passage on the ocean; and being moreover encouraged by her, I left my late peaceful home (in my sixtieth year) in search of personal security and those rights which by the laws of God I ought to have enjoyed undisturbed there and embarked at Beverly on board the schooner *Lively*, Captain Johnson, bound hither, on Sunday the 23rd ultimo and have just arrived. Hoping to find an asylum among the Quakers and Dutchmen, who I presume from former experience have too great a regard for ease and property to sacrifice either at this time of doubtful disputation on the altar of an unknown goddess, or rather doubtful divinity. . . .

My townsman, Benjamin Goodhue, was kind enough to come on board and, having made my kinsman and correspondent, Samuel Smith, acquainted with my arrival, he was pleased to come on board also; and his first salutation, "We will protect you, though a Tory," embarrassed me not a little. But soon recovering my surprise, we fell into a friendly conversation, and he taking me to his house, I dined with his family and their minister, Mr. Sprout, suffering some mortification in the cause of truth. After an invitation to make his house my home during my stay here, which I did not accept, I took leave and went in pursuit of lodgings and, on inquiring at several houses, ascertained they were full or for particular reasons would not take me; and so many refused as made it fearful whether, like Cain, I had not a discouraging mark upon me or a strong feature of Toryism. The whole city appears to be deep in congressional principles and inveterate against "Hutchinsonian Addressers." Happily, we at length arrived at one Mrs. Swords', a widow lady, in Chestnut Street, with whom I found quarters.

Saw Pelatiah Webster, who at the instance of Mr. Goodhue treats me civilly. Having had several intimations that my residence here would be unpleasant, if allowed at all, when it shall be known that I am what is called "an addresser" . . . I have, therefore, consulted the few friends I think it worthwhile to advise with and on the result am determined to proceed to London in the vessel in which I came here.

## A PHILADELPHIA TORY SUGGESTS THAT ENGLAND
## USE MORE MILITARY FORCE, 1776 [8]

You would hardly conceive, without seeing it, to what a height
the political fury of this country is arrived. I most heartily wish
myself at home among freeborn Englishmen, not among this tyrannical and arbitrary rabble of America. They have made many pro-
testations of respect for England, and of their desire of union with
the Mother Country; but you may take my word for it, my dear
friend, it is the meanest and basest hypocrisy that ever was assumed.
I have had occasion to spend, for a few years past, much of my time
in this province; and you may depend upon it, (and I am sure I
have neither interest nor wish to deceive you) that the present
breach with England is not the device of a day, and has not risen
with the question about taxation, (though that has been a favorable plea) but is part of a system which has been forming here, even
before the late war. You would feel the indignation I do every day,
when I hear my King and country vilified and abused by a parcel of
wretches, who owe their very existence to it. I am amazed at the
stupor and supineness of your Admiralty. For God's sake what are
you doing in England? Are the friends of Great Britain and their
property to be left exposed at this rate, to the dictates of an inhuman rabble? I expect, with many others, if I do not join in the
seditious and traitorous acts in vogue, to be hauled away and confined in a prison with the confiscation of all I have in the world.
Words cannot paint the distress of sober people who have property,
and wish for peace and quietness.

Where is the boasted Navy of our country, that only one poor
sloop is stationed here? Whereas if we had but three ships of war,
one of fifty and two of forty guns each, this place would not only
be kept in awe, and the friends of Government secured, but a sufficient quantity of provisions might be had at all times for your fleet
and army, which, we are informed, are half starved at Boston. As
to the sloop we have here, the Nautilus, I fear she will soon go to
the shades; for our friends are building above fifty row boats of
large dimensions, which are to have a twenty-four pounder in the
stern sheets, several swivels in the sides, and plenty of muskets for
the people on board, and for all the purposes of attacking the

[8] A letter from Philadelphia, August 1, 1775, in the *London Chronicle;* reprinted in Margaret W. Willard, ed., *Letters on the American Revolution, 1774–
1776* (Port Washington, New York, 1968), pp. 179–83.

King's ships that may arrive here. But if Government would order the Navy to sink all these vessels to the bottom whenever they met with them, a few examples of such timely severity would keep them on shore. I must not forget to tell you, that they are smuggling from the French West Indies in pilot boats all the ammunition they can get; but two or three cruisers off the Capes would soon put an end to that business.

Constant news arrives here, daily almost, which keeps up the mad enthusiasm of the people; namely, that an insurrection of thousands has begun in England; that Lord North is fled for his life to France or Italy; that Wilkes, Burke, Governor Johnstone, Lord Elfingham, Arthur Lee, and others, at the head of an armed multitude, had destroyed the Parliament House, and several members of the Administration. You would be amazed at the present rejoicing here upon this account. We are told likewise, that the Dutch have about fifty millions in our funds, and that they are about to demand them immediately, which will occasion a total bankruptcy to Great Britain. Everybody here believes this, and a hundred times as much more, for Gospel; which, I am well informed, is sent them by a set of people among you, whom humanity should teach not to sport thus with the lives and fortunes of these poor people here. All this increases the arrogance and ferment; and nobody dares to doubt it, unless he chooses to risk his life and substance; at least he must keep his doubts to himself. If this be liberty, Good Lord deliver me from all such liberty!

If government mean to do anything, they must do it quickly, or the contest will be the stronger. I am surprised you do not take and stop all the ships going in or coming out of these ports. Conceal my name; or I should run a great risk of my life and property, were it discovered here that I had sent you any account of these proceedings. Indeed, I incur some danger in writing at all; nor should I, if I could not confide in my conveyance.

### GOVERNOR JAMES WRIGHT OF GEORGIA ASKS FOR MILITARY ASSISTANCE, 1776 [9]

[The Rebels] say that now they have gone so far, that neither fortune nor lives are to be regarded, and that they will go every length. But still if we had proper support and assistance, I think

[9] Hezekiah Niles, ed., *Principles and Acts of the Revolution in America* (New York, 1876), pp. 226–27.

numbers would join the king's standard; but no troops, no money, no orders or instructions, and a wild multitude gathering fast, what can any man do in such a situation? No arms, no ammunition, not so much as a ship of war of any kind, and the neighboring Province at the same time threatening vengeance against the friends of government, and to send 1,000 men to assist the liberty people if they want assistance, all these things my Lord are really too much. They have also publicly declared that every man shall sign the association or leave the Province; that is, private persons, but that no King's officer shall be suffered to go: they will take care to prevent any of them from stirring. Surely my Lord, His Majesty's officers and dutiful and loyal subjects will not be suffered to remain under such cruel tyranny and oppression.

Your Lordship will judge of the cruel state and situation we are reduced to; the rebels encouraged and exulting; their numbers in and about town increased, according to the best information I can get, to about 800 men in arms; about 200 of their regiment or battalion already enlisted and daily increasing; a considerable part of my property seized upon, and the negroes employed in throwing up and making military works in and about the town; the King's officers and friends to government, some seized upon and kept prisoners, and others hiding and obliged to desert their families and property to save their lives and liberties, and some threatened to be shot whenever met with: which distresses my Lord I humbly conceive would not have happened, had no King's ships or troops come here, until there was sufficient to reduce the rebels at once.

## THE BRAVERY OF A MARYLAND TORY, DESCRIBED IN A LETTER TO ENGLAND, 1776 [10]

I could wish to speak more favorably of this colony, but a disposition to the full as repugnant to the rights of Great Britain, has been manifested here, as in the province of Massachusetts, only with less abilities to defend it, and less enthusiasm to carry it into execution. The first men, with respect to capacity and fortune, are on the side of government; but the rabble, which in this country as in every other, form by far the major part, often oblige them to be cautious and secret. Our Governor, notwithstanding his amiable qualities had secured to him the affections of the whole colony, is almost en-

---

[10] Extract of a letter from Maryland, January 12, 1776, in *Farley's Bristol Journal;* reprinted in Margaret W. Willard, ed., *Letters on the American Revolution, 1774–1776* (Port Washington, New York, 1968), pp. 252–54.

tirely deserted, and lives at Annapolis with his Secretary, and a very
few of his European friends. The mob have not done much mischief either on Patuxent or Potomac rivers, but they have showed a
brutality which proves the cause which they have unhappily
espoused to be both desperate and unjust.

Our old and valuable friend Mr. Lee, at Cedar Point, in the next
county, in a conversation relative to the Bostonians, inadvertently
damned them for destroying the tea. This was immediately made
public, and a mob of near 1500 or 2000 men assembled, and
marched to within three miles of his elegant house, from whence
they sent deputies to him; who, pretending to be his friends, and
that through their influence they had prevailed upon the mob to
stop, or they would have proceeded and laid his house level with
the ground, desired him, in order to appease their resentment, to
accompany them to where they were assembled, and sign a paper
retracting what he had said. His wife and daughters were by this
time apprised of the storm, and in fits. Yet, in this situation he left
his family, as the only means by which he could hope to save their
lives and his house, and accompanied by the rebel chiefs set out for
their associates. When he arrived, they gave him an instrument to
sign, and insisted on his going on his bare knees—when, to the
astonishment as well as confusion of them all, he manfully disdained
the slavish imposition.

"Take" (said our hoary and venerable friend) "the poor remains
of a life almost exhausted in your service. I have lived among you
upwards of seventy years, and with reputation; but if at this advanced age the malice of my enemies can drag me at their pleasure
from the peaceable enjoyments of domestic felicity; or if the blind
and uninformed rage of party, which contends for liberty and the
rights of humanity, at the very instant it is imposing the greatest
and most disgraceful of all slavery, *a restraint upon the mind,* can
with impunity triumph over natural justice, and force me to a concurrence in measures against the conviction of my conscience; it is
time to take an eternal farewell of the world. You may indeed kill
me, but you shall not force me to make an ignominious denial of
the truth, or to retract *one* syllable I have asserted."

"I have hitherto maintained through a variety of stations the
rights of my fellow-citizens; and acquainted as you all are with my
disposition, it can hardly be expected I would submit to a disgraceful surrender of my own. Act as you please; I have *lived a freeman,*
and it is my unalterable resolution to *die one.*" Upon which he
turned around, and left them in a profound silence, while he pur-

sued his journey home, uninterrupted by the *Sons of Liberty*, a they call themselves.

These outrages have not prevailed much among us, but this show to what cruelty and injustice they are capable of proceeding; and i also proves how far a manly fortitude will embarrass and confoun them. Mr. Lee has remained unmolested, and the rioters have bee universally condemned, even by their associates, for their brutality

### TORY SUFFERING IN NEW YORK, 1776 [11]

"The persecution of the loyalists continues unremitted. Don ald McLean, Theophilus Hardenbrook, young Fueter, the silve smith, and Rem Rapelje of Brooklyn, have been cruelly rode o rails, a practice most painful, dangerous, and till now, peculiar t the *humane* republicans of New England."

### THE NARRATIVE OF JOEL STONE OF CONNECTICUT, 1776–1778 [12]

In the year 1776 I discovered that it was perfectly impractica ble any longer to conceal my sentiments from the violent public The agents of Congress acted with all the cunning and cruelty o inquisitors and peremptorily urged me to declare without furthe hesitation whether I would immediately take up arms against th British Government or procure a substitute to serve in the genera insurrection.

I could no longer withhold any positive reply and unalterabl resolution of declining to fulfil their request by joining in an ac which I actually detested and which had been repeatedly deeme a rebellion by the public proclamation of General Howe. Th leader of the faction then informed me that my conduct in con sequence of such refusal would undergo the strictest scrutiny and that I might expect to meet the utmost severity to my person from those in authority and an incensed public.

Thus perpetually perplexed and harassed, I determined in my own mind to withdraw as soon as possible to the City of New York

[11] A letter dated "Staten Island, August 17, 1776"; in Edward Floyd De Lancey, ed., *History of New York during the Revolutionary War . . . by Thomas Jones* (New York, 1879), vol. 1, p. 597.

[12] James Talman, ed., *Loyalist Narratives from Upper Canada* (Toronto: The Champlain Society, 1946), pp. 323–29. Reprinted with the permission of the publisher.

and thereby joining his Majesty's forces cast what weight I was able into the opposite scale. But before I could carry my design into execution a warrant by order of the agents of Congress was issued out in order to seize my person. Being apprized of this and hearing that a party of men were actually on their way to my house, I packed up my books and bills, which I delivered to a careful friend to secrete, and left the care of my effects in the house to one of my sisters who had lived with me some time. Before the tumultuous mob which attended the party surrounded the premises, I had the good fortune to get away on horseback and, being in the dark night, happily eluded their search. But my sister, as I was afterwards given to understand, met the resentment of the mob, who from language the most opprobrious proceeded to actual violence, breaking open every lock in the house and seizing all the property they could discover. My goods and chattels thus confiscated they exposed to sale as soon as possible in opposition to the repeated remonstrances of my partner, declaring that the whole estate, real and personal, was become the property of the States.

But I soon found that my person was one principal object of their aim. Being informed to what place I had fled, a party of about twelve armed men with a constable came up and, seizing my horse, were proceeding into the house when I found an opportunity to slip from their hands. [It] was full fourteen days before I was perfectly secure, during which time several parties were detached after me, whom they were taught to consider as a traitor to the United States and unworthy to live. An invincible frenzy appeared to pervade the minds of the country people, and those very men who so recently had held one in the highest esteem became the most implacable enemies. I could not help considering my fate as peculiarly hard in thus being hunted as a common criminal and proscribed without cause in the very country that gave me birth, merely for performing my duty and asserting the rights of the British Constitution.

However, I had the unspeakable happiness to escape the utmost vigilance of my pursuers and at length reached Long Island. There I soon joined the King's army as a volunteer, in company with several gentlemen in the same persecuted situation, who also like myself had missed no opportunity of serving the royal cause but whose execution had been greatly curbed by the popular party. I remained thus until the 15th April, 1778, when, finding my money just expended amidst so many enormous calls and dreading that the patience of my best friends would not hold out much longer however willing they had been to assist me, I accepted a warrant to raise a company (as stated in my memorial presented to the Right Honorable the Lords Commissioners of His Majesty's Treasury), with a view to be in pay, especially as but little prospect was presented of a speedy termination being put to the unhappy war.

On the night of the 12th of May, 1778, as I was lying at Huntington on Long Island in order to carry my purpose of recruiting further into execution, I was surprised while asleep by a company of whale boatmen who took me prisoner and carried [me] over to Norwalk in Connecticut.

The magistrate before whom I was taken refused to consider me as a prisoner of war, which I claimed as a right, but charging me with the enormous crime of high treason against the States I was committed a close prisoner to Fairfield jail. I was there indicted, threatened with the vengeance of the law and warned solemnly for that death which most certainly would be inflicted upon me.

In a situation so perfectly horrible, perpetually exposed to the most barbarous insults of the populace and even some of the magistrates of the place, it may easily be supposed I would mediate [meditate] a recovery from a captivity so much to be dreaded. For a purpose so truly desirable I resolved to exert every effort of ingenuity that my mind could suggest. By the aid of my brother and other friends in that country I sent a flag to the commander of the king's army at or nigh King's Bridge in New York, soliciting immediate relief. This not producing the desired effect, I petitioned the Governor . . . that I might, agreeable to justice, be deemed a prisoner of war, treated as such and be permitted to appear before himself and Council in person to remove every objection to the late request. I freely offered to defray all the incidental expences occasioned by my removal across the country. However, he hesitated some time but at last agreed to my proposal. I paid for the strong guard which attended me by the way and entertained some hope of my meeting a favorable reception from the Governor.

The result turned out quite contrary to my wish. My petition was rejected with the utmost disdain and I was reminded to prepare for that approaching fate which was irrevocably fixed, as I was afterwards informed by a decree which could not be thwarted.

On my return the captain and guard buoyed me up by the way with a distant view of clemency, which in a great measure prevented me from an attempt which by the aid of pecuniary means must have freed me from so dreadful a situation, as I discovered that these mercenaries were far from being invulnerable in the respect alluded to. But as that must have cost me a considerable sum, the notion that

should one day be exchanged soothed for the present my perturbed
mind and prevented my immediate attempt to escape. But on my
return to prison all my sanguine hopes vanished and left my mind in
the utmost agitation. I began to renew my contrivances and in-
trigues in conjunction with my friends and resolved to spare no expense in my power to regain my liberty. Many of my schemes, though
they cost large sums, proved unsuccessful, yet I did not despair of
gaining my point. The dungeon was truly dismal, the walls strong
and the place perpetually guarded, yet being in the prime of life
my spirits were warm and my passions violent. I therefore firmly
determined to effect an escape if I even should be obliged to sink
the last shilling and go out naked into the world.

Communicating my final resolution to . . . a fellow prisoner, he
readily approved of my plan and embraced the offered opportunity
of being again free. By the generous aid of my friends and a judi-
cious application of almost all the money I could raise we happily
emerged from that place of horror July 23, 1778, and with quick
despatch pursued our way into the wilderness of that country to
wait the further assistance of our friends.

## PETER VAN SCHAACK OF NEW YORK TO THE
## PROVINCIAL CONVENTION, 1777 [13]

I am now about setting out, conformably to the sentence of
your Committee, to make the town of Boston my prison, to which
I am condemned by them unheard, upon a charge of *maintaining
an equivocal neutrality in the present struggles.* How far the punishment of banishment for this can be justified, either by the practice of
other nations, or upon those principles on which alone legitimate
governments are founded, and how far it answers those ends, which
alone make punishments a lawful exercise of power, I shall not at
present inquire; but as it implies, that your committee considers me
as a *subject* of your State, it behooves me, gentlemen, "to address
you with that freedom which can never give offense to the representatives of a free people."

When I appeared before the Albany committee, I refused to answer the question, whether I considered myself as a subject of Great
Britain, or of the State of New York, because I perceived the dilemma in which it would involve me, of either bringing punishment
on myself, in consequence of my own declaration, or of taking an

[13] January 25, 1777, in Henry C. Van Schaack, *The Life of Peter Van Schaack*
New York, 1842), pp. 71–76.

oath, which, if I had been never so clear respecting the proposition it contains, under the circumstances it was offered to me, and in m present situation, I should not have taken.

The reasons peculiar to myself, I shall not urge; but, supposin the independency of this State to be clearly established, I conceive i is premature, to tender an oath of allegiance before the governmen to which it imposes subjection, the time it is to take place of th present exceptionable one, and who are to be the rulers, as well a the mode of their appointment in future, are known; for with ever favorable allowance to those arguments which suppose it improba ble that those who are contending for the rights of mankind wil ever invade them, and that those who have vindicated libert against one tyranny, will establish or countenance another; I say admitting these arguments to have *weight,* both history and expe rience have, however, convinced me that they are by no means *con clusive.*

In the resolutions of the Provincial Congress of the 31st May last I find it declared, that *"many and great inconveniences* attend th mode of government by congress and committees, as of necessity in many instances, legislative, executive and judiciary powers hav been vested in them." Now, gentlemen, the union of these power in the same body of men, according to him whom the continenta congress call the "immortal Montesquieu," "puts an *end to liberty;*" and is there not cause, therefore, (reasoning entirely from the fal libility of mankind without respect to persons,) to be very jealous o a government, established by a body of men with such a plentitude of power, especially when they have not given the public the com mon security of an oath for the fair and impartial exercise of it? Have not the people a right to expect that the intended constitution should be published for their approbation, before they are com pelled, under so severe a penalty as banishment, to swear fidelity to it?

The declaration of independency proceeded upon a supposition that the constitution under which we before lived was actually dis solved, and the British government, as such, totally annihilated here. Upon this principle, I conceive that we were reduced to a state of nature, in which the powers of government reverted to the people, who had undoubtedly a right to establish any new form they thought proper; that portion of his natural liberty which each in dividual had before surrendered to the government, being now re sumed, and to which no one in society could make any claim until he incorporated himself in it.

But, gentlemen, admitting there was never so clear a majority in favor of independency, and who were convinced that they were absolved from their allegiance, and admitting that you are now vested with powers to form a new government, by the suffrages of a majority of the people of this State; permit me to observe that those who are of different sentiments, be they ever so few, are not absolutely concluded, in point of right thereby. The question whether a government is dissolved and the people released from their allegiance, is, in my opinion, a question of morality as well as religion, in which *every man* must judge, as he must answer for himself; and this idea is fairly held up to the public in your late address, wherein you declare, "that every individual must one day answer for the part he now acts." If he must *answer* for the part he acts, which certainly presupposes the right of private judgment, he can never be justifiable in the sight of God or man, if he acts against the light of his own conviction. In such a case no majority, however respectable, can decide for him.

But, admitting that a man is never so clear about the dissolution of the old government, I hold it that *every individual* has still a right to choose the State of which he will become a member; for before he surrenders any part of his natural liberty, he has a right to know what security he will have for the enjoyment of the residue, and "men being by nature free, equal and independent," the subjection of any one to the political power of a State, can arise only from "his own consent." I speak of the formation of society and of a man's initiating himself therein, so as to make himself a member of it; for I admit, that when once the society *is* formed, the majority of its members undoubtedly conclude the rest.

Upon these principles, I hold it that you cannot justly put me to the alternative of choosing to be a subject of Great Britain, or of this State, because should I deny subjection to Great Britain, it would not follow that I must necessarily be a member of the State of New York; on the contrary, I should still hold that I had a right, by the "immutable laws of nature," to choose any other State of which I would become a member. And, gentlemen, if you think me so dangerous a man, as that my liberty at home is incompatible with the public safety, I now claim it at your hands as my right, that you permit me to remove from your State into any other I may prefer, in which case, I reserve to myself the power of disposing of my property by sale or otherwise.

I would not be so far misunderstood, as if I supposed that no person is amenable to the authority of a State, unless he has expressly recognized and consented to it. I am aware, that there may be an implied consent arising from a temporary residence in a community and "deriving protection from the laws of the same." But, to make a man a member of any society, and a subject of its government, in that sense which would restrain him from quitting it, and removing to another he may like better, I conceive that a positive, express, unequivocal engagement is necessary. I am constrained, therefore, to deny, in its full latitude, the assertion in your resolution of the 16th July, "that persons *abiding* in the State and deriving protection from the *laws* of the same, are members of the state," for I hold it, that they are from those circumstances merely, no otherwise members of it than in a sense so qualified as to make the position immaterial in the present case. These, as far as I understand them, are the sentiments of Mr. Locke and those other advocates for the rights of mankind, whose principles have been avowed and in some instances carried into practice, by the Congress.

According to these principles I have endeavored to conduct myself during the present calamities of this country. Whatever my private opinions may have been of their rectitude, wisdom, or policy, I have acquiesced in the proceedings of the Congress, and expected whenever I transgressed their ordinances, to undergo the penalty, whether of fine, imprisonment, or otherwise; and this I conceived entitled me to *protection*. Between protection and reward in society, I conceived there was a wide difference, and that the man who took no active part against you, was entitled to the former, but that a claim to the latter could only be founded on some positive merit; and as I never solicited *favors*, I never expected to suffer for wanting the qualifications necessary to entitle me to them.

Disposed, however, to make allowances for the exigencies of the times, I would cheerfully have submitted to an abridgment of my liberty, if those in authority really thought it incompatible with the public safety; but then, in determining this, I expected regard should have been paid to the principles of judicial equity, and that those who gave an *opinion* respecting my principles, should have been compelled to assign the facts on which it was founded, and that I should have had an opportunity of controverting them, and of impeaching the credibility, or proving the infamy of the informers against me. But if I was to be condemned on suspicion, I expected at least that my informers and judges should have been under oath; and if a test was necessary, I expected it would be in consequence of some *general law*, putting all men who are in the same class in the same situation, and not that it should be left at he discretion of particular men to tender it to such individuals as malevolence, or party, family, or personal resentment should point out.

I have been several times apprised, that my brothers and myself have been represented to you as dangerous persons, whose influence has disseminated a general disaffection through the district, upon which charge I shall be silent, as I well know the invidious light in which declarations tending to remove suspicions of this nature are received. I cannot, however, avoid sending you a detail of the proceedings relative to this district, in which perhaps you will be able to trace a cause for its general disaffection, (if it be so,) more efficacious than any influence we can be supposed to have. An inquiry into this cannot be unworthy of your attention, and if you find an *adequate* cause in them, I hope all conjectures about a *supposed* one will vanish. With this detail you would sooner have been furnished, but that complaints of the abuses of power, are supposed in these cases to be levelled at the *power itself,* and imputed to an insidious view of exciting disunion.

I have now, gentlemen, concluded the business of this application, which, as I had not the honor of a personal hearing, I am obliged to offer by way of letter. My request is for leave to quit your State, and my reasons I have explained at large.

If my principles are ill-founded, or misapplied, I shall readily retract my errors when pointed out; but if they are founded on the immutable laws of nature, and the sacred rights of mankind, if they are such as are generally acknowledged by writers of the greatest eminence, and if they are necessarily connected with the same principles on which the American opposition is justified, I trust they will readily be admitted by you, though urged by an individual; nor do I conceive they now come before you in an extra-judicial way, but are clearly connected with my defense, on a charge which has been thought of importance enough to subject me to banishment from my native place.

## THE DIARY OF JAMES ALLEN OF PENNSYLVANIA, 1777 [14]

My particular situation has been of late very uneasy, owing to the battalion of militia of this district, assembling in the town of Northampton, to the number of 600 men . . . They are generally disorderly, being under no discipline; and I was particularly ob-

[14] Diary of James Allen, Esq., of Philadelphia, February 17, 1777, *Pennsylvania Magazine of History and Biography* (1885), pp. 288–89.

noxious, on account of my political opinions, and the conduct of my brothers, but particularly for the late assault I made on the Lieutenant Colonel when my chariot was attacked and which the whole battalion highly resented. Eight or nine parties of 15 or 20 men each came to demand blankets, one party of which, was very uncivil. But by prudence I escaped without any insult, having parted with 10 blankets. The principal officers behaved with great civility and the Colonel Boehm whom I had the encounter with, came to my house, to assure me he was innocent of the attack on my chariot and we buried the affair in oblivion. He assured me, that the soldiers were ripe for doing some violence to my house, which he with difficulty prevented, and upon the whole I had great good fortune to escape without some injury from a riotous incensed soldiery, and am at present pretty easy on that head. Notwithstanding this I am uneasy and wish to be in Philadelphia. My wife is often alarmed; I am afraid to converse with persons here, or write to my friends in Philadelphia, and a small matter, such as a letter intercepted or unguarded word, would plunge me into troubles. I never knew, how painful it is to be secluded from the free conversation of one's friends, the loss of which cannot be made up by any other expedients. I am considering whether I shall not leave this place in May and adjourn to Philadelphia. . . .

Oppressions multiply and it seems determined to make this country intolerable to all who are not actively its friends. The most discreet, passive, and respectable characters are dragged forth and though no charge can be made, yet a new idea is started, (which like all other beginnings of oppressive schemes soon become general) of securing such men as hostages. This circumstance makes me think my brothers happily out of the way. I daily expect, notwithstanding my present parole, to be further harassed, as I am extremely obnoxious. . . . These oppressions on men who have never given offence are justified by the Whigs as necessary for the security of all government; while the Tories think, that few cases can happen, where men of virtue ought innocently to [be] persecuted.

## LOYALISTS PETITION THE KING OF ENGLAND, 1782 [15]

The humble and dutiful declaration and address of his majesty's American loyalists, to the king's most excellent majesty, to both houses of parliament and the people of Great Britain.

[15] Hezekiah Niles, ed., *Principles and Acts of the Revolution in America* (New York, 1876), pp. 495–96.

We, his majesty's most dutiful and faithful subjects, the loyal inhabitants of America, who have happily got within the protection of the British forces, as well as those who, though too wise not to have foreseen the fatal tendency of the present wanton and causeless rebellion, yet, from numberless obstacles, the unexampled severities, have hitherto been compelled to remain under the tyranny of the rebels, and submit to the measures of congressional usurpation. . . .

The penalty under which any American subject enlists into his majesty's service, is no less than the immediate forfeiture of all his goods and chattels, lands and tenements; and if apprehended, and convicted by the rebels, of having enlisted, or prevailed on any other person to enlist into his majesty's service, it is considered as treason, and punished with death. Whereas, no forfeiture is incurred, or penalty annexed, to his entering into the service of congress; but, on the contrary, his property is secured, and himself rewarded.

The desultory manner also in which the war has been carried on, by first taking possession of Boston, Rhode Island, Philadelphia, Portsmouth, Norfolk in Virginia, Wilmington in North Carolina, etc., and then evacuating them, whereby many thousand inhabitants have been involved in the greatest wretchedness, is another substantial reason why more loyalists have not enlisted into his majesty's service, or openly espoused and attached themselves to the royal cause; yet, notwithstanding all these discouraging circumstances, there are many more men in his majesty's provincial regiments than there are in the continental service. Hence it cannot be doubted but that there are more loyalists in America than there are rebels; and also, that their zeal must be greater, or so many would not have enlisted into the provincial service, under such very unequal circumstances. . . .

Relying with the fullest confidence upon national justice and compassion to our fidelity and distresses, we can entertain no doubts but that Great Britain will prevent the ruin of her American friends, at every risk short of certain destruction to herself. But if compelled, by adversity of misfortune, from the wicked and perfidious combinations and designs of numerous and powerful enemies abroad, and more criminal and dangerous enemies at home, an idea should be formed by Great Britain of relinquishing her American colonies to the usurpation of congress, we thus solemnly call God to witness that we think the colonies can never be so happy or so free as in a constitutional connection with, and dependence on Great Britain; convinced, as we are, that to be a British subject, with all its consequences, is to be the happiest and freest member of any civil society in the known world—we, therefore in justice to our members, in duty to ourselves, and in fidelity to our posterity, must not, cannot refrain from making this public declaration and appeal to the faithful subjects of every government, and the compassionate sovereign of every people, in every nation and kingdom of the world, that our principles are the principles of the virtuous and free; that our sufferings are the sufferings of unprotected loyalty, and persecuted fidelity; that our cause is the cause of legal and constitutional government, throughout the world; that, opposed by principals of republicanism, and convinced, from recent observations, that brutal violence, merciless severity, relentless cruelty, and discretionary outrages are the distinguished traits and ruling principles of the present system of congressional republicanism, our aversion is unconquerable, irreconcilable; that we are attached to monarchical government, from past and happy experience—by duty, and by choice; that, to oppose insurrections, and to listen to the requests of people so circumstanced as we are, is the common interest of all mankind in civil society; that to support our rights, is to support the rights of every subject of legal government; and that to afford us relief, is at once the duty and security of every prince and sovereign on earth. . . .

### THE COST OF REMAINING LOYAL: LOYALIST CLAIMS MADE AND ALLOWED BY GREAT BRITAIN, 1785–88 [16]

First General Statement of Claims made by, and Losses liquidated of American loyalists:

**Losses of Property**

| Claims under the Acts of 1783 and 1785 | Number of Claims | Amount of Claims £ | s. | d. | Losses Allowed £ | s. | d. |
|---|---|---|---|---|---|---|---|
| 1. Loyalists who have rendered Services | 176 | 1,904,632 | 4 | 0 | 640,690 | 19 | 0 |
| 2. Loyalists who bore Arms in the service of Great Britain | 252 | 1,040,506 | 6 | 0 | 263,135 | 6 | 0 |
| 3. Loyalists zealous and Uniform | 414 | 1,744,492 | 18 | 0 | 531,616 | 4 | 0 |
| 4. Loyal British subjects resident in Great Britain | 31 | 342,139 | 4 | 0 | 140,927 | 0 | 0 |

[16] Edward Floyd De Lancey, ed., *History of New York during the Revolutionary War . . . By Thomas Jones* (New York, 1879), vol. 2, p. 660.

| Claims under the Acts of 1783 and 1785, cont. | Number of Claims | Amount of Claims | | | Losses Allowed | | |
|---|---|---|---|---|---|---|---|
| | | £ | s. | d. | £ | s. | d. |
| 5. Loyalists who took oaths to the Americans, but afterwards joined the British | 22 | 137,718 | 3 | 0 | 36,530 | 0 | 0 |
| 6. Loyalists who bore arms for the American States, but afterwards joined | 13 | 103,362 | 19 | 0 | 26,738 | 1 | 0 |
| 7. Loyalists sustaining losses under the Prohibitory Act, exclusive of others | 6 | 31,427 | 1 | 0 | 14,412 | 13 | 0 |
| 8. Loyal British Proprietors | 2 | 537,854 | 0 | 0 | 290,000 | 0 | 0 |
| 9. Loyalists now subjects or settled inhabitants of the United States, some of whom are persons of great merit | 21 | 51,578 | 0 | 0 | 20,077 | 0 | 0 |
| 10. Claims disallowed and withdrawn: | 243 | | | | | | |
| 1. Disallowed for want of proof of loyalty | (5) | 20,589 | 10 | 0 | | | |
| 2. Ditto for want of satisfactory proof | (189) | 653,819 | 3 | 0 | | | |
| 3. Ditto being fraudulent | (9) | 104,618 | 15 | 0 | | | |
| 4. Ditto being debts only | (16) | | | | | | |
| 5. Withdrawn | (24) | 145,582 | 12 | 0 | | | |
| 11. Loyal British Subjects, who appear to have relief provided for them by the Treaty of Peace | 2 | —— | | | 13,270 | 0 | 0 |
| N.B. The amount of the claims in these two cases is included in other classes. | | | | | | | |
| 12. Claims presented, but not prosecuted | 448 | 959,387 | 19 | 0 | | | |
| Claims under the Act of 1788 | | | | | | | |
| 13. Claim of John Penn, jun. and John Penn, sen. Esqs. (v. Special Report) | 1 | 944,817 | 8 | 6 | 500,000 | 0 | 0 |
| 14. Ditto of Lord Fairfax | 1 | 98,000 | 0 | 0 | 60,000 | 0 | 0 |
| 15. Ditto of the creditors on the ceded lands in Georgia | 11 | 45,885 | 17 | 5 | 45,885 | 17 | 5 |
| 16. Ditto of the other persons specially named in the Act of 1788 | 14 | 77,246 | 0 | 0 | 29,977 | 0 | 0 |
| | 1,657 | 8,943,657 | 19 | 11 | 2,613,260 | 0 | 5 |

## Losses of Income

| [Claims presented] | Number of Claims | Amount of Claims per annum | | | Loss of Income per annum found | | |
|---|---|---|---|---|---|---|---|
| | | £ | s. | d. | £ | s. | d. |
| Claims for loss of income allowed | 252 | 92,388 | 0 | 0 | 75,224 | 0 | 0 |
| Ditto of a person now a subject or settled inhabitant of the United States | 1 | 600 | 0 | 0 | 500 | 0 | 0 |
| Ditto where the parties have died since their claims were examined | 15 | 4,683 | 0 | 0 | 3,838 | 0 | 0 |
| Ditto which have been disallowed | 30 | 9,865 | 0 | 0 | | | |
| Ditto for loss of income allowed (referred by the Act of 1788) | 1 | 894 | 0 | 0 | 800 | 0 | 0 |
| | 299 | 108,430 | 0 | 0 | 80,372 | 0 | 0 |

# 3

# Tory Assessments of John Adams, George Washington, and the Rebel Forces

**LETTER OF A LOYALIST SURGEON, MAY, 1775** [1]

This [rebel] army, of which you will hear so much said, and see so much written, is truly nothing but a drunken, canting, lying, praying, hypocritical rabble, without order, subjection, discipline, or cleanliness; and must fall to pieces of itself in the course of three months, notwithstanding every endeavor of their leaders, teachers, and preachers, though the last are the most canting, hypocritical, lying scoundrels that this or any other country ever afforded. You are mistaken, if you think they are Presbyterian; they are Congregationalists, divided and subdivided into a variety of distinctions, the descendants of Oliver Cromwell's army, who truly inherit the spirit which was the occasion of so much bloodshed in your country from the year 1642 till the Restoration, but these people are happily placed at a distance from you, and though they may occasion a little expence of men and money before they are reduced to order, yet they cannot extend the calamities of war to your island. They have not been hitherto the least molested since the affair at Lexington. Time has been given for their passions to subside, but I do not suppose that the General's patience will continue much longer; he is at present confined to the town of Boston, and all supplies from the country stopped, and both the navy and the army live upon salt provisions of that sort; I am well informed, there are nine months provisions in the town.

---

[1] Margaret W. Willard, ed., *Letters on the American Revolution* (Boston, 1925), pp. 120–21.

## COMMENTS OF BENJAMIN THOMPSON, NOVEMBER 4, 1775 [2]

The [rebel] soldiers in general are most heartily sick of the service, and I believe it would be with the utmost difficulty that they could be prevailed upon to serve another campaign. The Continental Congress are very sensible of this, and have lately sent a committee to the camp to consult with the general officers upon some method of raising the necessary forces to serve during the winter season, as the greatest part of the army that is now in the field is to be disbanded upon the last day of December.

Whether they will be successful in their endeavors to persuade the soldiers to re-enlist or not, I cannot say, but am rather inclined to think that they will. For as they are men possessed of every species of cunning and artifice, and as their political existence depends upon the existence of the army, they will leave no stone unturned to accomplish their designs.

Notwithstanding the indefatigable endeavors of Mr. Washington and the other generals, and particularly of Adjutant General Gates, to arrange and discipline the army, yet any tolerable degree of order and subordination is what they are totally unacquainted with in the rebel camp. And the doctrines of independence and levellism have been so effectually sown throughout the country, and so universally imbibed by all ranks of men, that I apprehend it will be with the greatest difficulty that the inferior officers and soldiers will be ever brought to any tolerable degree of subjection to the commands of their superiors.

Many of their leading men are not insensible of this, and I have often heard them lament that the existence of that very spirit which induced the common people to take up arms and resist the authority of Great Britain, should induce them to resist the authority of their own officers, and by that means effectually prevent their ever making good soldiers.

Another great reason why it is impossible to introduce a proper degree of subordination in the rebel army is the great degree of equality as to birth, fortune and education that universally prevails among them. For men cannot bear to be commanded by others that are their superiors in nothing but in having had the good fortune to get a superior commission, for which perhaps they stood equally fair. And in addition to this, the officers and men are not only in

[2] The Historical Manuscripts Commission, *Report on the Manuscripts of Mrs. Stopford-Sackville* (London, 1904–1910), vol. 2, pp. 16–18.

general very nearly upon a par as to birth, fortune, etc., but in particular regiments are most commonly neighbors and acquaintances, and as such can with less patience submit to that degree of absolute submission and subordination which is necessary to form a well-disciplined corps.

Another reason why the army can never be well united and regulated is the disagreement and jealousies between the different troops from the different colonies; which must never fail to create disaffection and uneasiness among them. The Massachusetts forces already complain very loudly of the partiality of the General to the Virginians, and have even gone so far as to tax him with taking pleasure in bringing their officers to court martials, and having them cashiered that he may fill their places with his friends from that quarter. The gentlemen from the Southern colonies, in their turn, complain of the enormous proportion of New England officers in the army, and particularly of those belonging to the province of Massachusetts Bay, and say, as the cause is now become a common one, and the experience is general, they ought to have an equal chance for command with their neighbors.

Thus have these jealousies and uneasiness begun which I think cannot fail to increase and grow every day more and more interesting, and if they do not finally destroy the very existence of the army (which I think they bid very fair to do), yet must unavoidably render it much less formidable than it otherways might have been.

## PETER OLIVER ON JOHN ADAMS, 1776 [3]

Mr. Adams was born at a town, not far from Boston, of parentage not very distinguishable. It is generally supposed that he and Mr. Samuel Adams were nearly related; but I believe that there is no relation, either by affinity or consanguinity, except in their united endeavors in raising and supporting the present rebellion; and here, one soul informs both. Mr. John Adams was, also, educated at Harvard College in Cambridge; and after he was graduated, was employed as a schoolmaster to children of both sexes, in a country town. This employment is generally the porch of introduction to the sacred office, in New England; but Mr. Adams chose to pass from this porch by the same way he entered and try his genius

[3] Douglass Adair and John A. Schutz, eds., *Peter Oliver's Origin and Progress of the American Rebellion: A Tory View* (Stanford: Stanford University Press, 1961), p. 83. Reprinted with the permission of the Henry E. Huntington Library and Art Gallery, San Marino, California.

in the practice of law. He is a man of sense, and made a figure at the Bar; but whether nature had neglected him, or he had acquired, himself, an acrimony of temper by his . . . discipline, which he was remarkable for; certain it is, that acrimony settled into rancor and malignity—by having an absolute authority over children, he was determined to raise himself to a superiority which he had no claim to; and he unguardedly confessed, in one of his sallies of pride, that "he could not bear to see anyone above him." While he was young at the Bar, he behaved with great modesty; and as it is a general misfortune incident to gentlemen of the Bar, to brow-beat their inferiors, so, when any of his seniors took advantage of him in this way, the chief justice, Mr. Hutchinson, would, with his usual humanity, support him, as well as show him other marks of respect, out of court; but this chief justice, in a short time, found that there is no corner in a jealous, malignant heart for gratitude to creep into.

Mr. Adams, being a sensible lawyer, was for some time, friendly to government; but being in pursuit of a commission for the peace, Sir Francis Barnard, the then Governor, refused him. This refusal touched his pride, and from that time, resentment drove him into every measure subversive of law and of government, and interwove him with the factious Junto.

## NICHOLAS CRESSWELL ON GEORGE WASHINGTON, 1777 [4]

News that our army has surprised Washington and taken him prisoner. Afraid it is too good to be authentic. His great caution will always prevent him being made a prisoner to our inactive general. Washington is certainly a most surprising man, one of nature's geniuses, a heaven-born general, if there is any of that sort. That a Negro-driver should, with a ragged banditti of undisciplined people, scum and refuse of all nations on earth, so long keep a British general at bay, nay, even oblige him, with as fine an army of veteran soldiers as ever England had on the American continent, to retreat—it is astonishing. It is too much. By heavens, there must be double-dealing somewhere. General Howe, a man brought up to war from his youth, to be puzzled and plagued for two years together, with a Virginia tobacco planter. O! Britain, how thy laurels tarnish in the hands of such a lubber! The life of General Wash-

[4] *The Journal of Nicholas Cresswell, 1774–1777* (New York, 1924), pp. 251–57.

ington will be a most copious subject for some able biographer to exercise his pen upon. Nature did not make me one of the biographic order. However, I will make some remarks concerning this great and wonderful man.

George Washington, the American hero, was second son of a creditable Virginia tobacco planter (which I suppose may, in point of rank, be equal to the better sort of yeomanry in England). I believe his mother is still living and two of his brothers. . . . In the year 1755 he was chosen by the Assembly of Virginia to go to the French forts on the Ohio to know the reason why they made encroachments on the back parts of Virginia, which office he performed to the entire satisfaction of his employers. On his return he published his journal which did him great credit and first made him popular among his countrymen.

In the year 1754 the governor of Virginia gave him the command of about 1,000 troops (all Virginians), with orders to drive the French from their encroachments in the back settlements. In this expedition he proved unsuccessful. On the 3rd of July, 1754, he suffered himself to be surrounded by the French and Indians at the Big Meadows in the Allegheny Mountain and was obliged to capitulate, but upon what terms I do not recollect. He by some means or other got from the French very soon and had the command of a regiment of Virginians, and was with the unfortunate General Braddock when he was defeated by the French and Indians on the banks of the Monongahela River, July 9, 1755, prior to which he, with a part of his regiment, fell in with a scouting party of his own in the woods, an engagement began, and a number of men were killed before the mistake was discovered. He continued in the Army most of the war, but never performed any action to render himself conspicuous.

Before the expiration of the war he married a Mrs. Custis, a widow lady, with whom he had a very good fortune. By her entreaties he left the Army, in which he never gained any great esteem by his own country, officers or men. By all accounts it was his frugality that lost him the goodwill of his officers, and the strict discipline he always observed, the love of his men. Indeed, any kind of order or subordination ill agrees with his countrymen in general. After he quitted the Army, he was made a member of the Virginia House of Burgesses, in which he was much respected for his good private character, but always looked upon as too bashful and timid for an orator. He lived as a country gentleman, much noted for his hospitality, great knowledge in agriculture, and industry in carrying his various manufactories of linen and woolen to greater perfection than any man in the colony.

On the breaking out of these troubles he was chosen, in company with Messrs. Peyton Randolph, Richard Henry Lee, Patrick Henry, Richard Bland, Benjamin Harrison, and Edmund Pendleton, Esqs., to act as deputies or delegates for the colony of Virginia in the first Congress or Sanhedrin held at Philadelphia, September 5, 1774, and appointed general and commander in chief of all the rebel forces (by Congress) June 17, 1775. I believe he accepted this post with reluctance, but the great and almost unexpected success he has had may now soothe and become agreeable to his natural ambitious temper. He undoubtedly pants for military fame, and, considering the little military knowledge and experience he had before he was made a general, he has performed wonders. He was generally unfortunate (indeed I may with propriety say always) in every action where he was immediately concerned until the affair at Trenton in the Jerseys. Since that unlucky period (for us) he has only been too successful.

His education is not very great nor his parts shining, his disposition is rather heavy than volatile, much given to silence. In short, he is but a poor speaker and but shines in the epistolary way. His person is tall and genteel, age between forty and fifty, his behavior and deportment is easy, genteel, and obliging, with a certain something about him which pleases everyone who has anything to do with him. There cannot be a greater proof of his particular address and good conduct than his keeping such a number of refractory, headstrong people together in any tolerable degree of decorum. . . .

The general seems by nature calculated for the post he is in; he has a manner and behavior peculiar to himself and particularly adapted to his present station and rank in life. It is said (and I believe with great truth), that he never had an intimate, particular bosom friend, or an open professed enemy in his life. By this method of behavior he in a great measure prevents all parties and factions, and raises a spirit of emulation among his officers and men. As there is no favorite to pay their court to and pave their way to preferment, and the general, I believe, is proof against bribery, they have no advantage themselves but by merit alone. His private character is amiable; he is much beloved and respected by all his acquaintances.

From my personal acquaintance with him, and from everything that I have been able to learn of him, I believe him to be a worthy, honest man, guilty of no bad vice, except we reckon ambition among the number, and here we ought to judge charitably. The temptation was very great to a mind naturally ambitious. Nature made him too weak to resist it.

As an officer, he is quite popular, almost idolized by the southern provinces, but I think he is not so great a favorite with the northern ones. The ignorant and deluded part of the people look up to him as the savior and protector of their country, and have implicit confidence in everything he does. The artful and designing part of the people, that is, the Congress and those at the head of affairs, look upon him as a necessary tool to compass their diabolical purposes.

He certainly deserves some merit as a general, that he, with his banditti, can keep General Howe dancing from one town to another for two years together, with such an army as he has. Confound the great chucklehead, he will not unmuzzle the mastiffs, or they would eat him and his ragged crew in a little time were they properly conducted with a man of resolution and spirit. Washington, my enemy as he is, I should be sorry if he should be brought to an ignominious death.

## A LOYALIST ODE, 1778 [5]

Ye brave, honest subjects, who dare to be loyal,
And have stood the brunt of every trial,
   Of hunting-shirts, and rifle-guns:
Come listen awhile, and I'll sing you a song;
I'll show you, those Yankees are all in the wrong,
Who, with blustering look and most awkward gait,
'Gainst their lawful sovereign dare for to prate,
   With their hunting-shirts, and rifle-guns.

The arch-rebels, barefooted tatterdemalions,
In baseness exceed all other rebellions,
   With their hunting-shirts, and rifle-guns.
To rend the empire, the most infamous lies,
Their mock-patriot Congress, do always devise;
Independence, like the first of rebels, they claim,
But their plots will be damn'd in the annals of fame,
   With their hunting-shirts, and rifle-guns.

[5] Frank Moore, ed., *Songs and Ballads of the American Revolution* (New York, 1855), pp. 196–99.

Forgetting the mercies of Great Britain's king,
Who saved their forefathers' necks from the string;
   With their hunting-shirts, and rifle-guns.
They renounce allegiance and take up their arms,
Assemble together like hornets in swarms,
So dirty their backs, and so wretched their show,
That carrion-crow follows wherever they go,
   With their hunting-shirts, and rifle-guns.

With loud peals of laughter, your sides, sirs, would crack,
To see General Convict and Colonel Shoe-black,
   With their hunting-shirts, and rifle-guns.
See cobblers and quacks, rebel priests and the like,
Pettifoggers and barbers, with sword and with pike,
All strutting, the standard of Satan beside,
And honest names using, their black deeds to hide.
   With their hunting-shirts, and rifle-guns.

This perjured banditti, now ruin this land,
And o'er its poor people claim lawless command,
   With their hunting-shirts, and rifle-guns.
Their pasteboard dollars, prove a common curse,
They don't clink like silver and gold in our purse;
With nothing their leaders have paid their debts off,
Their honor's, dishonor, and justice they scoff,
   With their hunting-shirts, and rifle-guns.

For one lawful ruler, many tyrants we've got,
Who force young and old to their wars, to be shot,
   With their hunting-shirts, and rifle-guns.
Our good king, God speed him! never used men so,
We then could speak, act, and like freemen could go;
But committees enslave us, our Liberty's gone,
Our trade and church murder'd; our country's undone,
   By hunting-shirts, and rifle-guns.

Come take up your glasses, each true loyal heart,
And may every rebel meet his due desert,
   With his hunting-shirt, and rifle-gun.
May Congress, Conventions, those damn'd inquisitions,
Be fed with hot sulphur, from Lucifer's kitchens,
May commerce and peace again be restored,

And Americans own their true sovereign lord.
  Then oblivion to shirts, and rifle-guns.
    God save the King.

## ANN SEWARD DISPARAGES THE CHARACTER
## OF GEORGE WASHINGTON, 1781 [6]

Oh Washington! I thought thee great and good,
Nor knew thy Nero thirst for guiltless blood:
Severe to use the power that fortune gave,
Thou cool determined murderer of the grave.
Remorseless Washington! the day shall come
Of deep repentance for this barbarous doom;
When injured André's mem'ry shall inspire
A kindling army with resistless fire,
Each falchion sharpen that the Britons wield,
And lead their fiercest lion to the field;
Then, when each hope of thine shall end in night,
When dubious dread and unavailing flight
Impel your haste, thy guilt-upbraided soul
Shall wish, untouched, the precious life you stole;
And when thy heart, appalled and vanquished pride,
Shall vainly ask the mercy you denied,
With horror shalt thou meet the fate thou gave,
Nor pity gild the darkness of thy grave.

[6] Hezekiah Niles, ed., *Principles and Acts of the Revolution in America* (New York, 1876), p. 497.

# REBELS LOOK AT
# THE AMERICAN TORIES

*"It may be mentioned as a proof, both of the lenity of our government, and unanimity of its inhabitants,"* Thomas Jefferson recorded in his Notes on Virginia, *"that though this war has now raged some seven years, not a single execution for treason has taken place."* Perhaps the treatment of Tories was not as brutal as it might have been, given the high anger and calls for vengeance expressed by so many rebels against those neighbors who sided with Britain. And certainly there was less cruelty in this than in so many other fratricidal conflicts. Nevertheless, Jefferson's statement is wrong factually and questionable figuratively. Not many, but some executions for treason did take place. Nor was there ever any unanimity on how the rebel governments should deal with the Tories. Some demanded that they be put to death, or subject to severe punishment, or perpetually banished from America; others pled for moderation, leniency, and forbearance. There never was any consistent policy. The treatment of Tories varied according to time, place, and circumstance.

But on one issue virtually all rebels, from the most conciliatory to the most extreme, agreed: every individual had to make a choice. No neutrality could be tolerated. No mental reservations permitted. The apolitical, the ambiguous, the equivocal, all had to declare their sentiments for or against the revolution. *"He that is not a supporter of the independent states of America,"* Thomas Paine wrote at the beginning of the war, *". . . is, in the American sense of the word, A TORY."* And John Jay noted, after the fighting ended: *"I considered all who were not for us . . . as against us."* Thus, the rebels fashioned test oaths to force all indecisive characters—and there must have been many who wished to remain silent—to swear their fidelity to the cause of independence. In a revolution, according to one such oath, *"neutrality is not less base and criminal than open and avowed hostility."*

63

*The timid, the wary, the shrewd, were caught between British demands for fealty to the Crown, and rebel pressures to recognize the sovereignty of the independent states. Both sides practiced intimidation. One's declaration of loyalty frequently depended upon one's residence, and whether the British or the Americans were in control of that area. Many nominal Tories took the rebel oath. But those who could not or would not were confined to their homes, or farms, or isolated in particular regions; others were banished; thousands were fined; and the most suspicious were imprisoned. Non-jurors were subject to double and triple taxation. Many had their property sequestered. The rebels believed these measures to be justifiable, equitable, in fact indispensable; for in a civil war all must choose, the enemy must be identified and isolated—and punished according to the degree of his participation on Britain's side. But to the Tories the laws were both heinous and hypocritical, worse than any parliamentary enactment, a complete abrogation of the very freedoms which the rebels claimed to espouse.*

# 4

# Who Were the Tories? Rebel Definitions

## A PHILADELPHIA REBEL SPEAKS FOR AMERICA, 1776 [1]

The most ignorant amongst us sees to what shifts you are driven to justify your conduct. The *dignity of Great Britain,* the *supremacy* of *Parliament,* and such like ministerial jargon, produce nothing more than a smile of contempt. We are only surprised that while there are still some men who preside in your national Synod who are above corruption, that the promoters and supporters of such newfangled doctrines escaped being impeached of *treason*

---

[1] A letter from a gentleman of Philadelphia to his friend in London, May 18, 1776, in the *Gazetteer and New Daily Register*; reprinted in Margaret W. Willard, ed., *Letters on the American Revolution, 1774–1776* (Port Washington, New York, 1968), pp. 313–15.

*against the Constitution,* which we Americans look upon as the first and most dangerous species of rebellion. At sea, it is true, at present we are not upon a footing with you, but we soon shall be. We have four fine vessels in great forwardness here. . . . We have already powder sufficient to serve us seven years, allowing that you could export 50,000 hirelings to be slaughtered annually. In a word, my friend, it is not in the power of Great Britain to enslave us. Howe may possibly get possession of New York, and by way of doing *something,* may make a bonfire of it . . . but he will find himself in the same predicament that he found himself at Boston, and must soon be under the necessity of returning from whence he came. If he attempts to penetrate into the country, he will be attacked and beat. To talk of treating with him and his brigadiers, is a joke; it is ludicrous, and can only be meant to insult us. We will never submit till the bayonet is removed from our breasts to the scabbard, and your tyrannical Acts of Parliament are repealed.

Believe me, Sir, these are the sentiments of all degrees of men in British America, a few tattered Scotch Highlanders excepted, who have lately emigrated, and whose ignorance, feudal notions, and attachment *to names,* keeps them servile and wholly at the beck of their Chiefs. These, with a few Episcopalians from the same country, who are to a man Jacobites, are all that favor the cause of slavery and oppression. . . .

From what we have learned since General Washington took possession of Boston, though we have some Tories amongst us, Gage and Howe have full as many Whigs; and while your Ministry are fully determined to support the former, our Congress will not forget the latter.

## THE VIEW OF THOMAS PAINE, 1776 [2]

. . . What is a Tory? Good God! what is he? I should not be afraid to go with a hundred Whigs against a thousand Tories, were they to attempt to get into arms. Every Tory is a coward; for servile, slavish, self-interested fear is the foundation of Toryism; and a man under such influence, though he may be cruel, never can be brave. . . .

A person, to use a trite phrase, must be a Whig or a Tory in the

[2] Taken from Thomas Paine's *Crisis* papers, December 23, 1776, and April 19, 1777; reprinted in Daniel E. Wheeler, ed., *Life and Writings of Thomas Paine* (New York, 1908), vol. 3, pp. 7–8, 53–56.

lump. His feelings, as a man, may be wounded; his charity, as a Christian, may be moved; but his political principles must go through all the cases on one side or the other. He cannot be a Whig in *this* stage, and a Tory in *that*.

If he says he is against the united independence of the continent, he is to all intents and purposes against her in all the rest; because *this last* comprehends the whole. And he may just as well say, that Britain was right in declaring us rebels; right in taxing us; and right in declaring her *"right to bind the colonies in all cases whatsoever."* It signifies nothing what neutral ground, of his own creating, he may skulk upon for shelter, for the quarrel in no stage of it hath afforded any such ground; and either we or Britain are absolutely right or absolutely wrong through the whole.

Britain, like a gamester nearly ruined, hath now put all her losses into one bet, and is playing a desperate game for the total. If she wins it, she wins from *me* my life; she wins the continent as the forfeited property of rebels; the right of taxing those that are left as reduced subjects; and the power of binding them slaves; and the single die which determines this unparalleled event is, whether we support our independence or she overturn it. This is coming to the point at once.

Here is the touchstone to try men by. *He that is not a supporter of the independent states of America, in the same degree that his religious and political principles would suffer him to support the government of any other country, of which he called himself a subject, is, in the American sense of the word, A TORY; and the instant that he endeavors to bring his Toryism into practice, he becomes A TRAITOR.* The first can only be detected by a general test, and the law hath already provided for the latter. . . .

But there are certain species of Tories with whom conscience or principle hath nothing to do, and who are so from avarice only. Some of the first fortunes on the continent, on the part of the Whigs, are staked on the issue of our present measures. And shall disaffection only be rewarded with security? Can any thing be a greater inducement to a miserly man, than the hope of making his mammon safe?

And though the scheme be fraught with every character of folly, yet, so long as he supposes, that by doing nothing materially criminal against America on one part, and by expressing his private disapprobation against independence, as palliative with the enemy on the other part, he stands thereby in a safe line between both; while, I say, this ground be suffered to remain, craft, and the spirit of avarice, will point it out, and men will not be wanting to fill up this most contemptible of all characters.

These men, ashamed to own the sordid cause from whence their disaffection springs, add thereby meanness to meanness, by endeavoring to shelter themselves under the mask of hypocrisy; that is, they had rather be thought to be Tories from *some kind of principle,* than Tories by having *no principle* at all. But till such time as they can show some real reason, natural, political, or conscientious, on which their objections to independence are founded, we are not obliged to give them credit for being Tories of the first stamp, but must set them down as Tories of the last.

## CLASSES OF TORIES, CATEGORIZED BY BENJAMIN RUSH, 1777 [3]

I had frequent occasion to observe that the Tories and Whigs were actuated by very different motives in their conduct, or by the same motives acting in different degrees of force. The following classes of each of them was published by me in the early stages of the war, in Dunlap's paper. There were Tories (1) from an attachment to power and office. (2) From an attachment to the British commerce which the war had interrupted or annihilated. (3) From an attachment to kingly government. (4) From an attachment to the hierarchy of the Church of England, which it was supposed would be abolished in America by her separation from Great Britain. This motive acted chiefly upon the Episcopal clergy, more especially in the Eastern states. (5) From a dread of the power of the country being transferred into the hands of the Presbyterians. This motive acted upon many of the Quakers in Pennsylvania and New Jersey, and upon the Episcopalians in several of those states where they had been in possession of power, or of a religious establishment. . . .

Both parties differed as much in their conduct as they did in the motives which actuated them. There were (1) furious Tories who had recourse to violence, and even to arms, to oppose the measures of the Whigs. (2) Writing and talking Tories. (3) Silent but busy Tories in disseminating Tory pamphlets and newspapers and in circulating intelligence. (4) Peaceable and conscientious Tories who

[3] Rush's original classification of Tories was written in his 1777 Notebook; it was also published in a newspaper at that time. The above is taken from his later autobiographical writings in George W. Corner, ed., *The Autobiography of Benjamin Rush,* MEMOIRS of the American Philosophical Society, vol. 25 (1948), pp. 117–19. Reprinted with the permission of the publisher.

patiently submitted to the measures of the governing powers, and who showed nearly equal kindness to the distressed of both parties during the war. . . .

Perhaps the inhabitants of the United States might have been divided nearly into three classes, viz. Tories, Whigs, and persons who were neither Whigs nor Tories. The Whigs constituted the largest class. The 3rd class were a powerful reinforcement to them after the affairs of America assumed a uniformly prosperous appearance.

### NATHANIEL WHITAKER ON HOW TO RECOGNIZE A TORY, 1777 [4]

Observe the man who will neither go himself, nor contribute of his substance (if able) to encourage others to go into the war. Such do what in them lays to break up the army.

Others will express wishes for our success, but will be sure to back them with doubts of the event, and fears of a heavier yoke. You may hear them frequently magnifying the power of the enemy, and telling of the *nine hundred chariots of iron;* the dreadful train of artillery, and the good discipline of the *British* troops; of the intolerable hardships the soldiers undergo, and the starving condition of their families at home; and by a thousand such arts endeavoring to discourage the people from the war.

There are other pretended friends whose countenance betrays them. When things go ill with our army, they appear with a cheerful countenance, and assume airs of importance, and you'll see the core holding conferences in one corner or another. The joy of their hearts on such occasions, will break thro' all disguises, and discover their real sentiments; while their grief and long faces on a reverse of fortune, is a plain index pointing to the end at which they really aim.

Others, who talk much for liberty, you will find ever opposing the measures of defence proposed; making objections to them, and showing their inconsistency; while they offer none in their stead, or only such as tend to embarrass the main design. They are so prudent that they waste away days, yea months to consider; and are ever full of their wise cautions, but never zealous to execute any important project. These *over* and *over* prudent men ought to be suspected, and viewed with a watchful eye. And the discerning mind will soon be able to discover, whether such counsels spring from true wisdom, or from a design to ensnare.

[4] Nathaniel Whitaker, *An Antidote Against Toryism* (Salem, Massachusetts, 1811), pp. 20–25.

Some are discovered by the company they keep. You may find them often with those who have given too much reason to suspect their enmity to our cause, and rarely with the zealous friends of liberty, except by accident; and then they speak and act like creatures out of their element, and soon leave the company, or grow mute, when *liberty* is the subject of the discourse.

There are others who in heart wish well to our cause, but through fear of the power of our enemies they are backward to join vigorously to support it; they really wish we might succeed, but they dread the hardships of a campaign, and choose so to conduct, that on whatever side victory may declare, they may be safe.

Others wish well to the public cause, but have a much greater value for their own private and personal interest. They are high sons of liberty, till her cause crosses their private views, and even then they boast in her name, while like George III, they stab her to the heart, by refusing submission to those regulations which are essential to her preservation.


## A PHILADELPHIAN SUGGESTS PAINTING
## ALL TORIES BLACK, 1778 [5]

A correspondent in Philadelphia offers the following hint, with the hope that it will be improved upon:—"I have labored under many difficulties, for my principles are such, that I would not willingly purchase any article (except in absolute necessity) of a Tory. To be asking always who are Whigs who have to sell, is troublesome, and, I am sorry to say, uncertain. I wish the same mark were put upon the houses of our well-known enemies, as the Turks use to designate the residences of liars, that is, by painting them black. This might be done with a very small expense, and I am firmly convinced that every well-wisher to his country would willingly contribute towards paying the expense. The lower story blackened might be sufficient."

This suggestion, says another writer, does well enough as far as it goes, but we would propose a still more prominent designation of a Tory, that is, let the right side of the face and the right hand be dyed black, and if that don't answer, it will not be any great loss if the whole body be set to dying.

[5] From a colonial newspaper, August 22, 1778; reprinted in Frank Moore, ed., *Diary of the American Revolution* (New York, 1858), vol. 2, pp. 86–87.

# 5

# Rebel Opinions of Tories

## WHAT TO DO WITH A TORY MINISTER, 1774 [1]

*Hezekiah Huntington, Vine Elderkin, Ebenezer Gray,* and *John Ripley,* all of *Windham,* in the county of *Windham,* and Colony of *Connecticut,* of lawful age, testify and say, that on the 6th day of September, A.D. 1774, we, with other persons of this and some of the neighboring towns, went to *Hebron* to visit and deal with the Reverend *Samuel Peters,* of that place, for and on account of his making and publishing sentiments and principles incompatible with our civil liberties, subversive of our Constitution, and tending to make discord and dissension amongst the people at that critical time when a union was absolutely necessary. When we arrived at said Peters's house (which we found full of people, who were said to be armed) one Captain *Mack* came from the house and said that *Peters* desired the people to choose a committee to converse with him, which the people then accordingly did, of which we were part. . . . *Peters* then undertook to justify his conduct and principles, which consisted principally in trying to show that there was no duty laid without our consent, on the article of tea, because, he said, no man was obliged to buy, and when he did buy he consented to pay the duty, and so there could be no duty thereon if no man purchased it. The committee, after hearing him awhile, told him that their principles were fixed, and that they did not come there to dispute principles with him, and advised him to go out to the people, and perhaps he could convince them that he was right, which if he did, we would be satisfied, and assured him, on his request, that he should return into his house again safe, and without any abuse of any kind. (Antecedent to this said *Peters* declared that he had no arms in the house, except one or two old guns out of repair.) Upon which said *Peters* went out to the people, and being placed in the centre of a large number, he began to harangue the people as he did to the committee in the house; a few minutes after

[1] Peter Force, ed., *American Archives* (Washington, D.C., 1837–1853), Series IV: vol. 1, pp. 717–18.

a gun was discharged in the house, which much alarmed the people. Eight or ten people were immediately sent into the house to
know the occasion of the firing, and to see if there were any arms or
weapons of death therein, and found several guns and pistols loaded
with powder and ball, some swords, and about two dozen large
wooden clubs, concealed and hid in the house, and that the firing
was accidental, in which two balls were discharged from the gun
fired in the house; whereupon said eight or ten persons cleared the
house of all the men that were therein, and set sentinels at each door
of the house, that no damage might ensue, and thereupon, said
*Peters* having finished what he had to say to the people, which was
in no way satisfactory, the committee returned said *Peters* safely
into the house, and were ordered by the people to draw up something in writing, which said *Peters* should subscribe and acknowledge, which was accordingly done; and *Peters* likewise drew another, and thereupon, on the like assurances as before, *Peters* and
the committee went out to the people again, and *Peters,* according
to his desire, read what he wrote, which the people universally
rejected; and then the one drawn up by the committee was read
. . to the people and approved so far as was then wrote, which
*Peters* then absolutely refused to sign or acknowledge, although
urged and desired to do it by the committee, as they were afraid of
the consequences, as many of the people were warm and high, and
determined not to be delayed any longer; and thereupon the committee safely conveyed him into his house again, and were persuad-
ing him to sign the paper drawn up by the committee, as before-
said, when the people, impatient, weary, and hungry, would not be
put off or delayed longer, rushed into the house, by the door and
one window, (which was somewhat broken in the attempt) seized
and brought *Peters* out of the house, and placed him on a horse,
and carried him to the Meeting House Green, or Common Parade,
about three-quarters of a mile, where, after some talking upon the
premises, *Peters* agreed to, and did sign the paper, as was published,
and read it to the people himself; on which, they, with one voice, (to
appearance) accepted, and gave three cheers and dispersed. The
number of people was about three hundred. The sash of one window
of his house was broken, his gown and shirt somewhat torn, and it
was said by some that a table was turned over, and a punch bowl
and glass broken, which was all the damage that was done that we
ever heard of; and through the whole the committee endeavored to
calm and moderate the minds of the people, who were greatly ex-
asperated by Mr. *Peters's* conduct, firing the gun, preparing arms,

etc., as much as lay in their power; and also frequently told hi
that it was not for his religious sentiments, or because he was
church-man, or professed the religion established in the *Englis*
Nation, (before the Quebec Bill was passed) that we visited him, fc
some of the people were of that denomination, and that we were s
far from hurting or injuring any one that did profess it, that w
were ready to defend and protect them, when thereto called, wit
all our strength, but for the things and matters before mentione
we did visit him; and further these deponents say not.

## WHAT TO DO WITH A TORY JUDGE, 1775 [2]

We hear from Dutchess County, that on Saturday, the 16th i
stant, *James Smith*, Esq., a Judge of the Court of Common Ple
for that county, was very handsomely tarred and feathered for ac
ing in open contempt of the Resolves of the County Committee, a
was *Coen Smith*, of the same place, for like behavior. The Judg
undertook to sue for and recover the arms taken from the Tories b
order of said Committee, and actually committed one of the Con
mittee who assisted at disarming the Tories, which enraged th
people so much, that they rose and rescued the prisoner, and poure
out their resentment on this villainous retailer of the law.

## WHAT TO DO WITH A TORY COOPER, 1775 [3]

The 6th of December, at Quibble Town, Middlesex County
Pisquata Township, New Jersey, Thomas Randolph, Cooper, wh
had publicly proved himself an enemy to his country, by revilin
and using his utmost endeavors to oppose the proceedings of th
Continental and Provincial Conventions and Committees, in de
fence of their rights and liberties; and he being adjudged a perso
of no consequence enough for a severer punishment, was ordere
to be stripped naked, well coated with tar and feathers, and carrie
in a wagon publicly round the town—which punishment was ac
cordingly inflicted; and as he soon became duly sensible of his o

[2] A letter from Albany, New York dated September 27, 1775; in Edwar
Floyd De Lancey, ed., *History of New York during the Revolutionary War . .*
*by Thomas Jones* (New York, 1879), vol. 2, p. 591.

[3] Extract of a letter from New York, January 8, 1776, in *Daily Advertiser*; re
printed in Margaret W. Willard, ed., *Letters on the American Revolution, 1774-*
*1776* (Port Washington, New York, 1968), p. 251.

nce, for which he earnestly begged pardon, and promised to atone
far as he was able, by a contrary behavior for the future, he was
leased and suffered to return to his house in less than half an
our. The whole was conducted with that regularity and decorum,
at ought to be observed in all public punishments.

## DEATH TO ALL TORIES, 1776 [4]

I have often said that I supposed a Declaration of Independ-
ce would be accompanied with a declaration of high treason. Most
rtainly it must immediately, and without the least delay, follow
Can we subsist—did any state ever subsist, without exterminat-
g traitors? I never desire to see high treason extended here further
an it is now extended in Britain. But an act of high treason we
ust have instantly. The Colonies have long suffered inexpressibly
r want of it. No one thing made the Declaration of Independence
dispensably necessary more than cutting off traitors. It is amaz-
gly wonderful that, having no capital punishment for our intestine
emies, we have not been utterly ruined before now. For God's
ke, let us not run such risks a day longer! It appears to me, sir,
at high treason ought to be the same in all the United States, sav-
g to the legislature of each colony or state the right of attainting
dividuals by act or bill of attainder. The present times show
ost clearly the wisdom and sound policy of the common law in
at doctrine, or part thereof, which consists in attainting by an
t of the whole legislature. Our Tories (be sure the learned of
em) knew very well the absurdity of punishing as high treason
1y acts or deeds in favor of the government of the King of Great
ritain, so long as we all allowed him to be King of the Colonies.
This matter admits of no delay; and when the act declaratory of
igh treason is passed, the strongest recommendation for a strict
cecution of it, I humbly conceive, ought to accompany it. Our
hole cause is every moment in amazing danger for want of it. The
ommon understanding of the people, like unerring instinct, has
ng declared this; and from the clear discerning which they have
ad of it, they have been long in agony about it. They expect that
fectual care will now be taken for the general safety, and that all
10se who shall be convicted of endeavoring, by overt act, to destroy
1e state, shall be cut off from the earth.

[4] Joseph Hawley to Elbridge Gerry, July 17, 1776; reprinted in Peter Force, ed.,
*merican Archives* (Washington, D.C. 1848–1853), Series V: vol. 1, pp. 403–4.

## GEORGE WASHINGTON ON TORIES, 1776 [5]

All those who took upon themselves the style, and the title
government men in Boston, in short, all those who have acted a
unfriendly part in this great contest have shipped themselves off i
the same hurry, but under still greater disadvantage than the King
Troops have done; being obliged to man their own vessels (f
seamen could not be had for the transports for the King's use) an
submit to every hardship that can be conceived. One or two ha
done, what a great many ought to have done long ago, committe
suicide. By all accounts there never existed a more miserable set
beings, than these wretched creatures now are; taught to believe
that the power of Great Britain was superior to all opposition, an
that foreign aid (if not) was at hand, they were even higher, an
more insulting in their opposition than the Regulars. When th
order issued therefore for embarking the troops in Boston, no ele
tric shock, no sudden clap of thunder. In a word the last trum
could not have struck them with greater consternation. They we
at their wits' end, and conscious of their black ingratitude chose
commit themselves in the manner I have above described to th
mercy of the waves at a tempestuous season rather than meet the
offended countrymen. But with this declaration the choice was mad
that if they thought the most abject submission would procu
them peace they never would have stirred.

With respect to the Tory, who was tried and executed by you
order, though his crime was heinous enough to deserve the fate h
met with, and though I am convinced you acted in the affair with
good intention, yet I cannot but wish it had not happened. In th
first place, it was a matter that did not come within the jurisdictio
of martial law, and therefore the whole proceeding was irregular an
illegal, and will have a tendency to excite discontent, jealousy an
murmurs among the people. In the second, if the trial could prop
erly have been made by a court martial, as the division you con
mand is only a detachment from the army, and you cannot hav
been considered as in a separate department, there is none of ou
article[s] of War that will justify your inflicting a *capital* punish
ment, even on a soldier, much less a citizen. I mention these thing
for your future government, as what is past cannot be recalle

[5] George Washington to John A. Washington, March 31, 1776; reprinted i
John C. Fitzpatrick, ed., *The Writings of George Washington* (Washington, D.C
U.S. Government Printing Office, 1931–1944), vol. 9, pp. 6–7.

The temper of the Americans and the principles on which the present contest turns, will not countenance proceedings of this nature.

## A PLEA FOR LENIENCY, 1777 [6]

There will be a time and I hope it is not at a great distance when the distinction of Whig and Tory will be lost and resolve itself into the common appellation of *citizens of the Independent States*. All political grudges will die away and harmony and happiness cement the whole. I wish that no wound may be made among ourselves that time and common interest may not at last heal. In so great a convulsion sacrifices must be made but it has been the policy of every wise legislator to found the changes of government in lenity and forbearance.

## A CALL FOR VENGEANCE, 1779 [7]

Among the many errors America has been guilty of during her contest with Great Britain, few have been greater, or attended with more fatal consequences to these States, than her lenity to the Tories. At first it might have been right, or perhaps political; but is it not surprising that, after repeated proofs of the same evils resulting therefrom, it should still be continued? We are all crying out against the depreciation of our money, and entering into measures to restore it to its value; while the Tories, who are one principal cause of the depreciation, are taken no notice of, but suffered to live quietly among us. We can no longer be silent on this subject, and see the independence of the country, after standing every shock from without, endangered by internal enemies. Rouse, America! your danger is great—great from a quarter where you least expect it. The Tories, the Tories will yet be the ruin of you! 'Tis high time they were separated from among you. They are now busy engaged in undermining your liberties. They have a thousand ways of doing it, and they make use of them all. Who were the occasion of this war? The Tories! Who persuaded the tyrant of Britain to prosecute it in a manner before unknown to civilized nations, and shocking even to barbarians? The Tories! Who prevailed on the savages of the wilderness to join the standard of the enemy? The

[6] William Hooper to Robert Morris, February 1, 1777; in *Collections of the New York Historical Society for the year 1878* (New York, 1879), p. 418.

[7] *Pennsylvania Packet*, August 5, 1779; reprinted in Albert B. Hart, ed., *American History told by Contemporaries* (New York, 1912), vol. 2, pp. 474–76.

Tories! Who have assisted the Indians in taking the scalp from the aged matron, the blooming fair one, the helpless infant, and the dying hero? The Tories! Who advised and who assisted in burning your towns, ravaging your country, and violating the chastity of your women? The Tories! Who are the occasion that thousands of you now mourn the loss of your dearest connections? The Tories! Who have always counteracted the endeavors of Congress to secure the liberties of this country? The Tories! Who refused their money when as good as specie, though stamped with the image of his most sacred Majesty? The Tories! Who continue to refuse it? The Tories! Who do all in their power to depreciate it? The Tories! Who propagate lies among us to discourage the Whigs? The Tories! Who corrupt the minds of the good people of these States by every specie of insidious counsel? The Tories! Who hold a traitorous correspondence with the enemy? The Tories! Who daily sends them intelligence? The Tories! Who take the oaths of allegiance to the States one day, and break them the next? The Tories! Who prevent your battalions from being filled? The Tories! Who dissuade men from entering the army? The Tories! Who persuade those who have enlisted to desert? The Tories! Who harbor those who do desert? The Tories! In short, who wish to see us conquered, to see us slaves, to see us hewers of wood and drawers of water? The Tories!

And is it possible that we should suffer men, who have been guilty of all these and a thousand other calamities which this country has experienced, to live among us! To live among us, did I say? Nay, do they not move in on our assemblies? Do they not insult us with their impudence? Do they not hold traitorous assemblies of their own? Do they not walk the streets at noon day, and taste the air of liberty? In short, do they not enjoy every privilege of the brave soldier who has spilt his blood, or the honest patriot who has sacrificed his all in our righteous cause? Yes—to our eternal shame be it spoken—they do. Those very men who wish to entail slavery on our country, are caressed and harbored among us. Posterity will not believe it; if they do, they will curse the memory of the forefathers for their shameful lenity. Can we ever expect any grateful return for our humanity, if it deserves that name? Believe not a spark of that or any other virtue is to be found in the Tory's breast; for what principle can that wretch have who would sell his soul to subject his country to the will of the greatest tyrant the world at present produces? 'Tis time to rid ourselves of these bosom vipers. An immediate separation is necessary. I dread to think of the evils every moment is big with, while a single Tory remains among us.

May we not soon expect to hear of plots, assassinations, and every species of wickedness their malice and rancor can suggest? For what can restrain those who have already imbrued their hands in their country's blood? Did not that villain Matthews, when permitted to live among us at New York, plot the assassination of General Washington? He did; he was detected, and had he received his deserts, he would now have been in gibbets, instead of torturing our unfortunate friends, prisoners in New York, with every species of barbarity. Can we hear this, and still harbor a Tory among us? For my own part, whenever I meet one in the street, or at the coffee house, my blood boils within me. Their guilt is equalled only by their impudence. They strut, and seem to bid defiance to every one. In every place, and in every company, they spread their damnable doctrines, and then laugh at the pusillanimity of those who let them go unpunished. I flatter myself, however, with the hopes of soon seeing a period to their reign, and a total end to their existence in America. Awake, Americans, to a sense of your danger. No time to be lost. Instantly banish every Tory from among you. Let America be sacred alone to freemen.

Drive far from you every baneful wretch who wishes to see you fettered with the chains of tyranny. Send them where they may enjoy their beloved slavery to perfection—send them to the island of Britain; there let them drink the cup of slavery and eat the bread of bitterness all the days of their existence—there let them drag out a painful life, despised and accursed by those very men whose cause they have had the wickedness to espouse. Never let them return to this happy land—never let them taste the sweets of that independence which they strove to prevent. Banishment, perpetual banishment, should be their lot.

# 6

# The Problem of Controlling
# Tories in Wartime

### BRIGADIER-GENERAL JOHN SULLIVAN
### TO GEORGE WASHINGTON, 1775 [1]

That infernal crew of Tories, who have laughed at the Congress, despised the friends of liberty, endeavored to prevent fortifying this harbor, and strove to hurt the credit of the Continental money, and are yet endeavoring it, walk the streets here with impunity, and will, with a sneer, tell the people in the streets, that all our liberty-poles will soon be converted into gallows. I must entreat your Excellency to give some directions, what to do with those persons, as I am fully convinced, that if an engagement was to happen, they would, with their own hands, set fire to the town, expecting a reward from the ministry for such hellish service. Some, who have for a long time employed themselves in ridiculing and discouraging those, who were endeavoring to save the town, have now turned upon me, and are flying from one street to another, proclaiming that you gave me no authority to take the ships to secure the entrance of the harbor, or did any thing more than send me here, to see the town reduced to ashes, if our enemies thought proper. Sir, I shall wait your directions respecting these villains, and see that they are strictly complied with.

### HENRY FISHER TO THE COMMITTEE OF SAFETY
### IN DELAWARE, OCTOBER, 1776 [2]

On Monday last we held at this town an election for members of Assembly and Legislative Council, to represent this county in the General Assembly of the Delaware state, which day exhibited such a scene of disaffection to the common cause of America, as I think

[1] Written from Portsmouth, New Hampshire, October 29, 1775; reprinted in Jared Sparks, ed., *Correspondence of the American Revolution* (Boston, 1853), vol. 1, pp. 71–72.

[2] *Delaware Archives* (Wilmington, Delaware, 1919), vol. 3, p. 1367.

have not been equalled by any transaction on this continent since the commencement of the present dispute with Great Britain. The few friends of America in this county, almost worn out with perpetual contention, and convinced that further struggles were fruitless, determined for some time past not to concern in the election, and but very few of them came to town; the Tories, (for so I think I may justly call them,) flocked into the number of five and six hundred, pretty early in the day. At about 12 o'clock, one of them . . . came to me when setting at my own door, followed by a crowd, and demanded an ax to cut down the Liberty Pole standing in the street; and on my refusing, he seized me by the breast in order to drag me into the street. In a short time after they left me, they by some means procured an ax and went in a body to the pole and cut it down; when it fell, the streets resounded with huzzas for King George and General Howe, execrations against the Congress, Whigs, etc. They then took the top of the pole, on which part of the independent flag had been used to be hoisted, and carried it in derision about the town, followed by the crowd throwing up their hats and huzzaing for the King; and when tired with that kind of mockery, set it up at public sale, struck it off, it is said, for thirteen pence, meaning I suppose Hangman's wages. After this, one of their gang placed himself in the Court House door with a large hickory club, which he held across the door, saying every person who came in there should declare himself for the King, thus forcibly electing a number of their Junto to represent them in the General Assembly for this State; one of which has been disarmed by a committee of the late Assembly of this government as an enemy to the liberties of America, and another of whom has been convicted of being unfriendly to the common cause before the Committee of Safety of this county.

## A LOYALTY OATH FOR SUSPECTED TORIES IN RHODE ISLAND, 1776 [3]

I, ———, here, in the presence of Almighty God, as I hope for ease, honor, and comfort in this world, and happiness in the world to come, most earnestly, devoutly, and religiously do swear, that I will neither directly nor indirectly assist the wicked instruments of ministerial tyranny and villainy, commonly called the king's troops and navy, by furnishing them with provisions and refreshments of

[3] Edward Floyd De Lancey, ed., *History of New York during the Revolutionary War . . . by Thomas Jones* (New York, 1879), vol. 1, p. 572.

any kind, unless authorized by the Continental Congress or Legisla ture, at present established in this particular colony of Rhode Is land.

I do also swear, by the tremendous and Almighty God, that I wil neither directly nor indirectly convey any intelligence, nor give any advice to the aforesaid enemies described; and that I pledge myself if I should by any accident get knowledge of such treasons, to in form immediately the committee of safety.

And, as it is justly allowed that when the rights and sacred liber ties of a nation or community are invaded, neutrality is not less base and criminal than open and avowed hostility, I do further swear and pledge myself, as I hope for eternal salvation, that I will, when ever called upon by the voice of the Continental Congress, or by the Legislature of this particular colony under their direction, take up arms, and subject myself to military discipline in defence of the common rights and liberties of America. So help me God.

### APPLYING THE LOYALTY OATH ON LONG ISLAND, 1776 [4]

It is a duty that I owe to my Commander to acquaint him of my proceeding in executing the order he gave me. Yesterday after noon I arrived at Newtown, and tendered the oath to four of the grate Torries, which they swallowed as hard as if it was a four pound shot, that they ware trying to git down. On this day at 11 o'clock I came here, whare I sent out scouting parties, and have ben able to ketch but five Torries, and they of the first rank, which swallowed the oath. The houses are so scatering it is impossible to ketch many without hosses to rid after thim. But I shall exert myself to ketch the gratest part of the ringledors, and beleve I shell effect it, but not less then five days from this time. I can assure your honor they are a set of villins in this country, and beleve the better half of them are wateing for soport and intend to take up arms against us. And it is my opinion nothing else will do but removing the ringledors to a place of secuerty.

### PROCEEDINGS OF THE GENERAL ASSEMBLY HELD FOR THE COLONY OF RHODE ISLAND, JULY, 1776 [5]

Whereas, Messrs. Joseph Wanton, Jr., Mathew Cozzens, John Haliburton, William Hunter, Samuel Gibbs, Silas Cook, Jr., An-

[4] Isaac Sears to General Charles Lee, March 17, 1776, in *Ibid.*, vol. 1, p. 573.
[5] John R. Bartlett, ed., *Records of the Colony of Rhode Island* (Providence, Rhode Island, 1862), vol. 7, pp. 593–94.

thony Lechmere, Christopher Hargill, Augustus Johnston, Andrew Christie and Joseph Farrish, have refused, and still refuse, to subscribe the test, or declaration, prescribed by an act of the Assembly, tendered to them, agreeably to said act; It is therefore voted and resolved, that the persons above named, be, by the sheriff of the county of Newport, removed at their own expense, to the following places, viz.:

Col. Joseph Wanton to be removed to the town of Jamestown, and have the liberty of that town, under the inspection of the commander in chief at Rhode Island, and that he be permitted, whenever the said commander in chief shall think proper, to pass under a guard, to visit his farm on Prudence; but to no other place, whatever, off the Island of Connecticut.

That Augustus Johnston, be removed to the town of South Kingstown.

That Mathew Cozzens, be removed to Cumberland.

John Haliburton, to Hopkinton.

William Hunter, to Smithfield.

Samuel Gibbs, to Scituate, north of Plainfield Road.

Silas Cook, Jr., to South Kingstown.

Anthony Lechmere, to Glocester.

Christopher Hargill, to Cumberland.

Andrew Christie, to North Kingstown.

Joseph Farrish, to Cumberland.

And that they continue within the limits of the said towns, and support themselves, therein; excepting the said Samuel Gibbs, who is to continue within the limits before mentioned.

That if either of said persons transgress said limits, they be immediately apprehended and committed to jail, within the county to which they are removed; and if either of said persons shall refuse to pay the expense of their removal, and for their support in said towns, that the same shall be allowed by this State; and that their estates be immediately seized to, and for the use of the state, and their persons immediately confined in the jail within the county where they are removed.

## WASHINGTON'S PROCLAMATION, 1777 [6]

Whereas several persons, inhabitants of the United States of America, influenced by inimical motives, intimidated by the threats

[6] Proclamation of January 25, 1777, in Frank Moore, ed., *Diary of the American Revolution* (New York, 1858), vol. 1, pp. 383–84.

of the enemy, or deluded by a proclamation issued the 30th of No
vember last, by Lord and General Howe, styled the King's Commis
sioners for granting pardons, etc., (now at open war, and invading
these States) have been so lost to the interest and welfare of their
country, as to repair to the enemy, sign a declaration of fidelity,
and in some instances have been compelled to take the oaths of al
legiance, and engage not to take up arms, or encourage others to dc
so, against the King of Great Britain: And whereas it has become
necessary to distinguish between the friends of America and those of
Great Britain, inhabitants of these States, and that every man whe
receives protection from, and is a subject of any State, (not being
conscientiously scrupulous against bearing arms) should stand ready
to defend the same against hostile invasion: I do, therefore, in be
half of the United States, by virtue of the powers committed to me
by Congress, hereby strictly command and require every person,
having subscribed such declaration, taken such oaths, and accepted
such protection and certificate, to repair to headquarters, or to the
quarters of the nearest general officer of the Continental army or
militia, (until further provision can be made by civil authority) and
there deliver up such protection, certificate, and passports, and
take the oath of allegiance to the United States of America; nevertheless, hereby granting full liberty to all such as prefer the interest
and protection of Great Britain to the freedom and happiness of
their country, forthwith to withdraw themselves and families
within the enemy's lines. And I do hereby declare, that all and
every person who may neglect or refuse to comply with this order,
within thirty days from the date hereof, will be deemed adherents
to the King of Great Britain, and treated as common enemies of
these American States.

### THE ADVICE OF SAMUEL ADAMS, 1777 [7]

A few days ago a small expedition was made under the authority of this State, aided by a detachment of Continental Regulars
to suppress the Tories in the counties of Somerset and Worchester
on the eastern shore of Chesapeake, where they are numerous and
have arisen to a great pitch of insolence. . . . In my opinion, much

[7] Samuel Adams to James Warren, February 16, 1777; reprinted in Harry A.
Cushing, ed., *The Writings of Samuel Adams* (New York, 1907), vol. 3, pp. 360–61.

more is to be apprehended from the secret machination of these rascally people, than from the open violence of British and Hessian soldiers, whose success has been in a great measure owing to the aid they have received from them. You know that the Tories in America have always acted upon system. Their headquarters used to be in Boston—more lately in Philadelphia. They have continually embarrassed the public councils there, and afford intelligence, advice and assistance to General Howe. Their influence is extended throughout the United States. Boston has its full share of them and yet I do not hear that measures have been taken to suppress them. On the contrary, I am informed that the citizens are grown so polite as to treat them with tokens of civility and respect. Can a man take fire into his bosom and not be burned? Your Massachusetts Tories communicate with the enemy in Britain as well as New York. They give and receive intelligence from whence they early form a judgment of their measures. . . . Indeed, my friend, if measures are not soon taken, and the most vigorous ones, to root out these pernicious weeds, it will be in vain for America to persevere in this glorious struggle for the public liberty.

### ROBERT R. LIVINGSTON, MATTHEW CANTINE, AND ZEPHANIAH PLATT TO THE PRESIDENT OF THE PROVINCIAL CONVENTION OF NEW YORK, 1777 [8]

SIR: We find the number of [Tory] conspirators infinitely greater than we could have conceived; almost everybody in the Upper Manor (as it is sometimes called), particularly the eastern part of it, appears to have been engaged with the enemy, first by taking an oath of secrecy, and then an oath of allegiance to the King of Great Britain; it appears to have been their design to have waited till the enemy came up, when they were to rise and take the whigs prisoners. We think it absolutely necessary that a court martial should be organized here tomorrow out of the offices of the Manor of Claverack and Rhinebeck regiments, for the trial of some few of the principal offenders. An act of grace should be prepared, though not yet issued, and a proper place provided for at least two hundred prisoners, and provision be made for their maintenance.

[8] Letter dated May 8, 1777; in Edward Floyd De Lancey, ed., *History of New York during the Revolutionary War . . . by Thomas Jones* (New York, 1879), vol. 2, pp. 411–12.

## COLONEL WILLIAM RICHARDSON TO THE COMMISSIONERS
## OF THE BOARD OF WAR IN PHILADELPHIA, 1777 [9]

From the best information I have been able to collect, and from my own observations it appears that a large majority of the inhabitants of this county [Sussex County, Delaware] are disaffected; and would I believe afford the enemy every aid in their power, except personal service in the field, which the greater part of them want spirit to do. They are a set of poor, ignorant, illiterate people, yet they are artful and cunning as foxes, 'tis hardly possible to detect the most open offenders, yet they are almost every day offending. I have had several of the most open and daring before me, but upon examination nothing has been proved against them that would justify my keeping them prisoners. I have read the Oath of Allegiance proposed in the assembly of this state to them, and they declare they are willing to take it. I should therefore be glad to be empowered to administer that or such a one as Congress may judge proper to be taken by these rascals; for to apprehend, and turn them loose again, with only a reprimand, serves rather to harden than to convince or convert them.

## AN ACT MORE EFFECTUALLY TO PREVENT THE MISCHIEFS,
## ARISING FROM THE INFLUENCE AND EXAMPLE OF PERSONS
## OF EQUIVOCAL AND SUSPECTED CHARACTERS, IN THIS STATE
## [NEW YORK]. PASSED THE 30TH OF JUNE, 1778 [10]

*Whereas* certain of the inhabitants of this state, have, during the course of the present cruel war, waged by the king and Parliament of Great Britain, against the people of these States, affected to maintain a neutrality, which there is reason to suspect was in many instances, dictated by a poverty of spirit, and an undue attachment to property. *And whereas* divers of the said persons, some of whom, advocated the *American* cause till it became serious, have notwithstanding the forebearance of their countrymen, and

[9] August 9, 1777; reprinted in George H. Ryden, ed., *Letters to and from Caesar Rodney, 1756–1784,* Historical Society of Delaware (Philadelphia: University of Pennsylvania Press, 1933), pp. 211–12n. Reprinted with the permission of the publisher.

[10] Victor H. Paltsits, ed., *Minutes of the Commissioners for detecting and defeating Conspiracies in the State of New York* (Albany, 1909–1910), vol. 2, pp. 783–86.

ontrary to the faith pledged by their paroles, ungratefully and
nsidiously from time to time, by artful misrepresentations, and a
ubtle dissemination of doctrines, fears and apprehensions false in
hemselves, and injurious to the *American* cause, seduced certain
veak minded persons from the duties they owed their country;
*And whereas* the welfare of this state, loudly demands that some de-
isive measures be taken with respect to the said persons; and it
peing repugnant to justice as well as good policy, that men should
pe permitted to shelter themselves under a government, which they
not only refused to assist in rearing, but which, some of them daily
endeavor to undermine and subvert; *And whereas*, such few of the
said persons, as may have been led to take a neutral part by conscientious doubts and scruples, have had more than sufficient time
to consider and determine the same;

I. *Be it enacted by the People of the State of New York, represented
in Senate and Assembly, and it is hereby enacted by the Authority
of the same,* That the Commissioners appointed for inquiring into,
detecting and defeating all conspiracies, which may be formed in
this State, against the Liberties of *America;* or any three of them
pe, and they hereby are authorized and strictly charged and required, to cause all such persons, of neutral and equivocal characters in this state, whom they shall think have influence sufficient to
do mischief in it, to come before them, and to administer to the
said persons respectively, the following oath, or if of the people
called Quakers, affirmation, *viz.*

> "I, A.B. do solemnly, and without any mental reservation or
> equivocation whatever, swear and call God to witness; or if of the
> people called Quakers, affirm, that I do believe and acknowledge,
> the state of *New York*, to be of right, a free and independent state.
> And that no authority or power, can of right, be exercised in or over
> the said state, but what is, or shall be granted by or derived from
> the people thereof. *And further,* That as a good subject of the said
> free and independent state of *New York*, I will to the best of my
> knowledge and ability, faithfully do my duty; and as I shall keep or
> disregard this oath. So help and deal with me Almighty God."

II. *And be it further enacted by the Authority aforesaid,* That if on
the said Oath or affirmation, being so tendered, the said person or
persons shall refuse to take the same, the said Commissioners do
forthwith remove the said person or persons so refusing, to any place
within the enemy's lines, and by writing under their hands and
seals, certify the names of such person or persons, to the Secretary of

this state, who is hereby required to record and file the said certifi
cates.

III. *And be it further enacted by the Authority aforesaid,* That i
any of the said neutrals, shall abscond or absent himself with a
apparent view to avoid the force of this act, the said Commissioner
shall by notice, published in one or more of the newspapers of thi
state, demand of the said person or persons, so absconding or ab
senting, to appear before them, at such place in this state, and a
such time, not exceeding twenty-one days from the time of such
publication, as they shall assign. *And further,* That default in such
appearance, shall be judged to amount to and is hereby declared to
be a refusal to take the said oath or affirmation.

IV. *And be it further enacted by the Authority aforesaid,* That i
any of the persons removed to places within the enemy's lines b
the said commissioners, in pursuance of this act, or who havin
as aforesaid, absconded or absented, shall not on notice as afore
said appear before the said Commissioners, and take the oath or af
firmation aforesaid, shall thereafter be found in any part of thi
state; such person or persons so found, shall on conviction thereof
be adjudged guilty of misprison or treason.

*And to the End,* That this state may be in some measure compen
sated for the injuries it has sustained, by the evil example or prac
tices of the said neutrals, and that others may be deterred on simi
lar occasions, from acting a part so unmanly and ignominious;

V. *Be it further enacted by the Authority aforesaid,* That all land
held in this state, on the twenty-sixth day of *June* Instant, in fe
simple or fee tail, or which may hereafter be acquired by, or devised
granted, or descend to any of the Persons who shall refuse to take
the aforesaid oath or affirmation, when called upon by the said
Commissioners, shall forever thereafter, be charged with double
taxes, in whosoever hands the said lands may hereafter be.

VI. *And be it further enacted by the Authority aforesaid,* That the
said Commissioners, previous to the removal of the said several per
sons within the enemy's lines, shall from time to time, notify the
person administering the government of this state for the time
being, of the several persons so to be removed, who is hereby au
thorized to detain and confine, such of the said persons as he shal
think proper, for the purpose of exchanging them for any of the
subjects of this state, in the power of the enemy.

VII. *And be it further enacted by the Authority aforesaid,* That
the person administering the government of this state for the time

being, be, and he is hereby required to do his best endeavors, that this act be fully and speedily carried into execution, and all magistrates, sheriffs, and constables, are required to be aiding therein.

## MINUTES OF THE COMMISSIONERS FOR DETECTING AND DEFEATING CONSPIRACIES IN THE STATE OF NEW YORK: ALBANY COUNTY SESSIONS, 1778–81 [11]

*April 20, 1778.* Adam Vrooman appearing before this board, and charged with going off to the enemy, but no proof appearing that he had taken an active part against the States and he being willing and offered to take the Oath of Allegiance, was thereupon permitted to return upon bail to his place of abode.

*May 1, 1778.* Daniel Campbell Esquire and James Ellice were brought before the Board for speaking words that in the opinion of the board might have a dangerous tendency and prove detrimental to the liberties of America. Ordered that they be respectively held in recognizance in £500 each.

*May 25, 1778.* John Sealy who was confined for going to the enemy was brought before us and we having examined him and judging from his appearance that he had been seduced by others from his allegiance: ordered that he be permitted to go at large on entering into recognizance for good behavior and monthly appearance.

*June 9, 1778.* Jacob Cluet was apprehended for uttering sentiments unfavorable to the American cause and for insinuating that he knew of and was accessory to plots and conspiracies formed and concerted by the Tories and was brought before us and we having examined the persons who were brought as evidences against him: ordered that the said Jacob Cluet be permitted to return home on his entering into recognizance for good behavior and appearance next Friday eight days.

*July 18, 1778.* Benjamin Morrison was apprehended as a suspicious person and we having examined him and finding from a paper in his possession that he holds a correspondence with the enemy, and that he in the state of Connecticut has always borne the character of a disaffected character: ordered that he be closely confined.

*September 7, 1778.* Alexander Campbell of Schenectady who was adjudged in the opinion of this board a person of a neutral and

[11] *Ibid.,* vol. 1, pp. 91, 102, 126, 140, 174, 225, 243, 260, 279, 289, 306, 373, 430; vol. 2, pp. 454, 624.

equivocal character and was in consequence thereof cited to appear before the Board, appeared and the Oath being tendered him as prescribed in the Act lately passed by the Legislature he refused to take the same and requested from the Board permission to go to Canada with his family: which request was granted him.

*September 25, 1778.* William Smith of the Manor of Renselaerwyck appeared before the Board and complained of Samuel Rock as being a person inimical to the American cause and dangerous to the safety of the state. Ordered that Major Barent Staats be requested to have the said Samuel Rock apprehended and sent to us.

*October 19, 1778.* Andries Ten Eyck and Jacob Legrange who were allowed time to consider of the Oath prescribed to be taken by persons of neutral and equivocal character appeared and the Oath being tendered them they severally refused to take the same. Ordered that they hold themselves in readiness to be removed within the enemies lines on the shortest notice.

*November 5, 1778.* [There was] laid before the Board two papers, the one being a remonstrance . . . by George White Esquire and a number of other persons setting forth that Aaron Hammond the person therein mentioned is a person disaffected to the cause of America and praying that he may not be permitted any longer to keep a tavern; the other being a recommendation from a number of persons in favor of the said Aaron Hammond.

*November 25, 1778.* George White Esquire who was cited to appear before the Board to support the charge of Toryism by him alleged against Aaron Hammond this day appeared and informed us that he compromised the matter with the said Aaron Hammond and that it was settled in such a manner as was satisfactory to both.

*January 5, 1779.* Whereas it has been represented to this Board that George Herchemer of Tryon County has been restricted to his farm by William Wells Esquire under a pretence of disaffection to the American cause and it appearing to us from sundry circumstances that the going at large of the said George Herchemer will not endanger the safety of the state: therefore resolved that the said George Herchemer have permission to go at large until the further order of this board.

*June 29, 1779.* Joseph Concklin of New Town having been apprehended for declaring that he was a friend to the King of Great Britain and making use of other expressions which plainly evinced his disaffection to the American cause and being brought before the Board: resolved that he be committed.

*December 31, 1779.* The Board having received information that
saac Lamb of the Manor of Renselaerwyck who joined Burgoyne's
rmy in the year 1777 is lately come from the enemy and is now
t his former place of abode: resolved that a warrant be made out
or the immediate apprehension of the said Isaac Lamb.

*July 10, 1780.* Edward Archer of this city appeared before the
oard and informed [us] that George Rodgers did yesterday in his
resence say that the French fleet was come to carry off the damned
ebel officer Washington, who was afraid he would be hanged; that
he Whigs were all a set of scoundrels and rascals; and that he was
ersuaded the British troops would in a fortnight's time march
hrough the city of Albany.

*January 29, 1781.* Hannah Bemus, wife of Jotham Bemus, having
een ordered to appear before the Board, appeared this day agree-
ble to the said order and being interrogated as to Angus McDonald
f Livingston's Manor carrying on an intercourse with the enemy,
nd harboring British officers who are passing through the country
s expresses, and she refusing to answer to the same, and there being
reat reason to suppose that she is acquainted with the above cir-
umstances: therefore resolved that she be committed until she gives
atisfactory answers.

## THE CONVICTION AND PENALTY OF SEAGOE POTTER
## FOR TREASON IN DELAWARE, 1780 [12]

The jurors for the Delaware state upon their oath present,
hat Seagoe Potter, being an inhabitant and subject of the Delaware
tate and owing allegiance to the government thereof, not having
he fear of God in his heart but being moved and seduced by the
nstigation of the Devil as a false rebel and traitor to the said state
nd devising and most wickedly and traitorously intending to
hange and subvert the rule and government of the said state and
educe the same to the domination of the King of Great Britain, on
he eighth day of August in the year of our lord one thousand seven
undred and eighty and at divers other days and times as well be-
ore as after at Broadkill, Broad Creek and Dagsbury hundreds, and
t divers other places in the county aforesaid, with a great multi-
ude of other traitors and rebels to the said state (to the jurors un-
nown) being armed and arrayed in a warlike and hostile manner,
o wit: with guns, pistols, swords, clubs and divers other weapons, as

---

[12] *Delaware Archives* (Wilmington, Delaware, 1919), vol. 3, pp. 1302–4.

well offensive as defensive, with force and arms did falsely and tra
torously assemble and join themselves against the said state. . .
[The] aforesaid did go to the house of a certain Clark Nottingha
a Lieutenant in the Militia of the said state, and to the house
divers other liege inhabitants, and did falsely and traitorously ta
from the said houses a quantity of arms, powder and ball, in .
pursuance of their traitorous intentions and purposes. Well kno
ing that a great multitude of rebels and traitors to the said state we
in actual rebellion, [they] did falsely and traitorously aid and ass
the said rebels and traitors in actual rebellion by giving them i
telligence and furnishing them with arms, ammunition and pro
sions and other supplies against the duty of their allegiance, again
the peace and dignity of the Delaware state, and against the for
of an Act of General Assembly in such case made and provided. . .

The jurors being elected, tried and sworn, say on their oath th
Seagoe Potter is guilty of the treason and felony whereof he stan
indicted. . . . The said Seagoe Potter is immediately asked if
has or knows anything to say for himself, why the said court he
should not proceed to judgment and execution thereof upon t
verdict, who nothing further says than as before he had sa
Whereupon all and singular the premises being seen, and by t
Court here understood, it is considered by the Court that you, Se
goe Potter, return to the prison from whence you came, from then
you must be drawn to the place of execution. When you come the
you must be hanged by the neck but not till you be dead, for yc
must be cut down alive, then your bowels must be taken out, a
burnt before your face, then your head must be severed from yo
body, and your body divided into four quarters, and these mu
be at the disposal of the Supreme Authority of the State.

# 7

## Post-War Attitudes
## Towards Tories

### JOHN JAY TO PETER VAN SCHAACK, 1782 [1]

I felt very sensibly for you and for others, but as society can regard only the political propriety of men's conduct, and not the moral propriety of their motives to it, I could only lament your unavoidably becoming classed with many whose morality was convenience, and whose politics changed with the aspect of public affairs. My regard for you as a good old friend continued, notwithstanding. God knows that inclination never had a share in any proceedings of mine against you; from such thorns no man could expect to gather grapes, and the only consolation that can grow in their unkindly shade is a consciousness of doing one's duty and the reflection that, as on the one hand I have uniformly preferred the public weal to my friends and connections, so on the other I have never been urged by private resentments to injure a single individual. Your judgment and consequently your conscience differed from mine on a very important question; but though, as an independent American, I considered all who were not for us, and you among the rest, as against us, yet be assured that John Jay did not cease to be a friend to Peter Van Schaack. No one can serve two masters. Either Britain was right and America wrong, or America was right and Britain wrong. They who thought Britain right were bound to support her, and America had a just claim to the services of those who approved her cause. Hence it became our duty to take one side or the other, and no man is to be blamed for preferring the one which his reason recommended as the most just and virtuous. Several of our countrymen left and took arms against us, not from any such principles, but from the most dishonorable of human motives. Their conduct has been a piece with their inducements, for they have far out-stripped savages in perfidy and cruelty. Against

[1] September 17, 1782; reprinted in Henry P. Johnston, ed., *The Correspondence and Public Papers of John Jay* (New York, 1891), vol. 2, pp. 343–45.

these men every American must set his face and steel his heart. There are others of them, though not many, who, I believe, opposed us because they thought they could not conscientiously go with us. To such of them as have behaved with humanity I wish every species of prosperity that may consist with the good of my country.

### REBEL FEELING IN NEW YORK: TWO LETTERS
### AND A NEWSPAPER ITEM, 1783 [2]

(1) The British are leaving New York every day. Last week there came one of the damned Refugees from New York to a place called Wall-Kill, in order to make a tarry with his parents, where he was taken into custody immediately; his head and eyebrows were shaved, tarred and feathered, a hog yoke put on his neck, and a cowbell thereon; upon his head a very high cap of feathers was set, well plum'd with soft tar, and a sheet of paper in front, with a man drawn with two faces, representing Arnold and the Devil's imps; and on the back of it a card with the refugee or tory driving her off.

(2) By our latest accounts from New York we understand the tories are in great perplexity. . . . And from the associations which are formed by the whigs they could expect nothing but rough handling the moment that the citizens were assembled. Such of the old tory party who remain will be the first objects of the popular rage, and the apostates who signed the association in 1775 and afterwards joined the British, with the traders and other strangers who have gone into New York in the course of the war, will be noticed in their order. Such, as I am informed, is the intention of the old citizens, and if it is necessary, they will be supported by their friends from the Country; so that if any considerable number of obnoxious characters continue in the City after the British give it up, there will be great confusion for a while, but no more than all things considered might be expected.

(3) The exiled Whigs present their most respectful compliments to Messieurs TORIES, and beg leave to inform those sticklers for *British* tyranny, that with heart-felt satisfaction the late suffering Whigs find the old proverb fully verified, 'After a storm comes a calm.' The Whigs take the liberty to prognosticate that the calm, which the enemies of Columbia at present enjoy, will ere long be succeeded by a bitter and *neck-breaking hurricane.*

² Edward Floyd De Lancey, ed., *History of New York during the Revolutionary War . . . by Thomas Jones* (New York, 1879), vol. 2, pp. 505–6.

## THE REBEL POET, PHILIP FRENEAU, WRITES A TORY'S EPISTLE UPON HIS DEPARTURE FOR NOVA SCOTIA, 1783 [3]

Dark glooms the day that sees me leave this shore,
To which fate whispers I must come no more:
From civil broils what dire disasters flow—
Those broils condemn me to a land of woe
Where barren pine trees shade the dreary steep,
Frown o'er the soil or murmur to the deep,
Where sullen fogs their heavy wings expand,
And nine months' winter chills the dismal land!
Could no kind stars have mark'd a different way,
Stars that presided on my natal day?
Why is not man endued with power to know
The ends and upshots of events below?
Why did not heaven (some other gift deny'd)
Teach me to take the true-born Buckskin side,
Show me the balance of the wavering fates
And fortune smiling on these new-born States!

Friend of my heart!—my refuge and relief,
Who help'd me on through seven long years of grief,
Whose better genius taught you to remain
In the soft quiet of your rural reign,
Who still despised the Rebels and their cause,
And, while you paid the taxes, damn'd their laws,
And wisely stood spectator of the fray,
Nor trusted George, whate'er he chose to say;
Thrice happy thou, who wore a double face,
And as the balance turn'd could each embrace;
Too happy Janus! had I shar'd thy art,
To speak a language foreign to my heart,
And stoop'd from pomp and dreams of regal state,
To court the friendship of the men I hate,
These strains of woe had not been penn'd to-day,
Nor I to foreign climes been forc'd away:
Ah! George—that name provokes my keenest rage,
Did he not swear, and promise, and engage
His loyal sons to nurture and defend,

[3] Fred L. Pattee, ed., *The Poems of Philip Freneau* (New York, 1963), vol. 2, p. 219–23.

To be their God, their father and their friend—
Yet basely quits us on a hostile coast,
And leaves us wretched where we need him most:
His is the part to promise and deceive,
By him we wander and by him we grieve;
Since the first day that these dissentions grew,
When Gage to Boston brought his blackguard crew,
From place to place we urge our vagrant flight
To follow still this vapor of the night,
From town to town have run our various race,
And acted all that's mean and all that's base—
Yes—from that day until this hour we roam,
Vagrants forever from our native home!

And yet, perhaps, fate sees the golden hour
When happier hands shall crush rebellious power,
When hostile tribes their plighted faith shall own
And swear subjection to the British throne,
When George the Fourth shall their petitions spurn,
And banish'd Tories to their fields return.

From dreams of conquest, worlds and empires won
Britain awaking, mourns her setting sun,
No rays of joy her evening hour illume,
'Tis one sad chaos, one unmingled gloom!
Too soon she sinks unheeded to the grave,
No eye to pity and no hand to save:
What are her crimes that she alone must bend?
Where are her hosts to conquer and defend—
Must she alone with these new regions part,
These realms that lay the nearest to her heart,
But soar'd at once to independent power,
Not sunk like Scotland in the trying hour?
See slothful Spaniards golden empires keep,
And rule vast realms beyond the Atlantic deep;
Must we alone surrender half our reign,
And they their empires and their worlds retain?
Britannia, rise—send Johnstone to Peru,
Seize thy bold thunders and the war renew,
Conquest or ruin—one must be thy doom,
Strike—and secure a triumph or a tomb!

But we, sad outcasts from our native reign,
Driven from these shores, a poor deluded train,
In distant wilds, conducted by despair,

Seek, vainly seek, a hiding place from care!
Even now yon' tribes, the foremost of the band,
Crowd to the ships and cover all the strand:
Forc'd from their friends, their country, and their **God,**
I see the unhappy miscreants leave the sod!
Matrons and men walk sorrowing side by side
And virgin grief, and poverty, and pride,
All, all with aching hearts prepare to sail
And late repentance that has no avail!
While yet I stand on this forbidden ground
I hear the death-bell of destruction sound,
And threat'ning hosts with vengeance on their **brow**
Cry, "Where are Britain's base adherents now?"
These, hot for vengeance, by resentment led,
Blame on our hearts the failings of the head;
To us no peace, no favors they extend,
Their rage no bounds, their hatred knows no end;
In one firm league I see them all combin'd,
We, like the damn'd, can no forgiveness find—
As soon might Satan from perdition rise,
And the host angels gain their vanish'd skies
As malice cease in their dark souls to burn,
Or we, once fled, be suffer'd to return.

   Curs'd be the union that was form'd with France,
I see their lillies and the stars advance!
Did they not turn our triumphs to retreats,
And prove our conquests nothing but defeats?
My heart misgives me as their chiefs draw near,
I feel the influence of all potent fear,
Henceforth must I, abandon'd and distrest,
Knock at the door of pride, a beggar guest,
And learn from years of misery and pain
Not to oppose fair Freedom's cause again!—
One truth is clear from changes such as these,
Kings cannot always conquer when they please,
Nor are they rebels who mere freedom claim,
Conquest alone can ratify the name—
But great the task, their efforts to control
When genuine virtue fires the stubborn soul;
The warlike beast in Lybian deserts plac'd
To reign the master of the sun-burnt waste,
Not tamely yields to bear a servile chain,

Force may attempt it, and attempt in vain,
Nervous and bold, by native valor led,
His prowess strikes the proud invader dead,
By force nor fraud from freedom's charms beguil'd
He reigns secure the monarch of the wild.

## AEDANUS BURKE OF SOUTH CAROLINA, 1783 [4]

The proceedings of the late Assembly have already excited the attention not only of this but of other States; and some of the laws then enacted are of so serious a nature, that the memory of them will last, and their consequences operate, when the authors of the measures shall be no more. By one of those laws, upwards of two hundred men who have been citizens of this State before the reduction of Charlestown, have been stripped of all their property; innocent wives and children, involved in the calamity of husbands and fathers, their widows are deprived of the right of dower, their children disinherited, and themselves banished forever from this country. And this *without process, trial, examination,* or *hearing,* and without allowing them the sacred right of proving their innocence on a future day. Under other acts of that assembly, a number of the inhabitants are subjected to heavy fines, some to near one third, others to one eighth and some to a tenth part of their estate, real and personal, without better proof of crime than report and suggestions. Another act excludes from the freedom of voting or being elected to a seat in the legislature, almost a majority of our citizens. The crimes of all consist in the part which they were said to have taken after the reduction of South Carolina by the British Army.

One would imagine there is no free country upon earth, in which laws bringing such ruin on so many families, and so big with political mischief, would not have been publicly discussed before this day. But whether it be owing, that the measures have succeeded in breaking the spirit of the people, by filling every man with a sense of his own danger; or that the fear of the Governor's *extraordinary power,* awes men into silence; or that they are indifferent about public affairs; not a man has yet undertaken to inquire into the justice or injustice of it, or ask his neighbor how far the Legislature could effect the ruin and disgrace of so many of his fellow

[4] Aedanus Burke ("Cassius"), *An Address to the Freemen of the State of South Carolina* (Philadelphia, 1783), pp. 3–6.

citizens, consistently with the laws, constitution, and happiness of his country.

### BENJAMIN FRANKLIN: WHO WAS MORE LOYAL TO AMERICA? 1785 [5]

We differ a little in our sentiments respecting the loyalists (as they call themselves), and the conduct of America towards them, which, you think, "seems actuated by a spirit of revenge; and that it would have been more agreeable to policy, as well as justice, to have restored their estates upon their taking the oaths of allegiance to the new governments." That there should still be some resentment against them in the breast of those, who have had their houses, farms, and towns so lately destroyed, and relations scalped under the conduct of these royalists, is not wonderful; though I believe the opposition given by many to their re-establishing among us is owing to a firm persuasion that there could be no reliance on their oaths; and that the effect of receiving those people again would be an introduction of that very anarchy and confusion they falsely reproach us with. . . .

The war against us was begun by a general act of Parliament declaring all our estates confiscated; and probably one great motive to the loyalty of the royalists was the hope of sharing in these confiscations. They have played a deep game, staking their estates against ours; and they have been unsuccessful. But it is a surer game, since they had promises to rely on from your government, of indemnification in case of loss; and I see your Parliament is about to fulfill those promises. To this I have no objection, because, though still our enemies, they are men; they are in necessity; and I think even a hired assassin has a right to his pay from his employer. It seems, too, more reasonable that the expense of paying these should fall upon the government who encouraged the mischief done, rather than upon us who suffered it; the confiscated estates making amends but for a very small part of that mischief. It is not, therefore, clear that our retaining them is chargeable with injustice.

I have hinted above, that the name *loyalist* was improperly assumed by these people. *Royalists* they may perhaps be called. But the true *loyalists* were the people of America, against whom they acted. No people were ever known more truly loyal, and universally so, to their sovereigns. The Protestant succession in the House of

Hanover was their idol. Not a Jacobite was to be found from one end of the colonies to the other. They were affectionate to the people of England, zealous and forward to assist in her wars, by voluntary contributions of men and money, even beyond their proportion. The king and Parliament had frequently acknowledged this by public messages, resolutions, and reimbursements. But they were equally fond of what they esteemed their rights; and they resisted when those were attacked. It was a resistance in favor of a British constitution, which every Englishman might share in enjoying, who should come to live among them; it was resisting arbitrary impositions, that were contrary to common right and to their fundamental constitutions, and to constant ancient usage.

### BENJAMIN FRANKLIN: ANALYSIS OF THE LOYALISTS, 1788 [6]

Two hundred and eighty-eight persons called Loyalists, and specified by name in the *Morning Post*, [should be] classed in the following manner:

| | |
|---|---:|
| Persons residing in Great Britain ........................... | 32 |
| Deceased persons ......................................... | 34 |
| Apostates, that is to say, who conformed to the American government, and voluntarily taken the necessary oaths, among whom also are divers who had been demagogues and leaders of the people, and who had reformed in hopes of saving their estates after the capture of Charlestown by Sir Henry Clinton, and who are now desirous of being [re-]reformed for the same benefit ................................................... | 139 |
| Persons of doubtful principle, viz., who, from the beginning, were endeavoring to play a safe game, and take the strongest side, as occasion might offer ............................. | 12 |
| Persons whose names are unknown, and others who are known to be of no weight or importance, the greatest part of whom would probably come under the title of Apostates .......... | 71 |
| | 288 |
| American True Loyalists ................................... | 000 |
| | 288 |

[6] *Ibid.*, vol. 10, pp. 72–73.

# HISTORICAL APPRAISALS
# OF THE AMERICAN TORIES

*The selections that follow are arranged chronologically, depending upon the time when each was written, and are meant to afford the reader a perspective of the historical treatment of Tories. The first two are really primary sources, contrasting accounts of the revolution by contemporaries. The work of David Ramsay of South Carolina, a member of Congress, was first printed in 1789 in Philadelphia and reprinted in London in 1793. It is remarkably insightful and temperate, though obviously partial to the rebel side. The work of Thomas Jones, a Loyalist who had been a judge of the Supreme Court of New York, was written after Jones went to England in the 1780s, and remained in manuscript form until its publication in 1879. It is a bitter work, filled with invective, but invaluable for its depictions of events as seen and known by a prominent Tory.*

*The rancor against Tories filled early histories of America. One such work, The Romance of the Revolution, referred to them as "blood-thirsty," and described the "hapless victims" of the Tories, who were subjected to "every means of torture that ingenuity could suggest. . . . Hanging, roasting over slow fires, or a pistol at the head, were the usual methods adopted." Mason Weems, in his enormously popular book about George Washington, offered a single explanation of why some Americans became Tories: their fear of Hessian brutality. "They burnt houses—destroyed furniture—killed the stock—abused the women! To save their families from such horrid tragedies, the Americans flocked in by the thousands to General Howe, to take the oath of allegiance." Only the figure of George Washington, firm "as the iron rudder-bands that maintain the course of the ship in her trembling flight over raging seas," saved the nation from destruction.*

*Not until the mid-nineteenth century do more balanced interpretations of the Tories appear. Henry C. Van Schaack in*

*1842 published a sympathetic account of his Loyalist father, but "not without apprehensions as to its reception." Lorenzo Sabine completed his revised study of the Loyalists during the Civil War. In it he attempted to explain similarities, as well as differences, between Rebel and Tory. In fact, the Civil War was instrumental in helping to alter American concepts of "loyalty" and "rebellion," and caused the public to rethink and to revise their image of the Tories. By the end of the century one finds in the work of John Fiske a sensitive and tactful summary of how the Tory issue was dealt with in the peace negotiations.*

*Included are excerpts from the writings of five modern scholars, sophisticated attempts to answer old questions about Tory behavior and motivations. L. F. S. Upton analyzes the make-up of a leading Tory, William Smith of New York and Quebec. Paul Smith deals with England's military use (or misuse) of the Tories. Leonard Labaree, Wallace Brown, and William Benton offer different keys to an understanding of the Tory character.*

## DAVID RAMSAY: A REBEL VIEW OF THE REVOLUTION [1]

In former ages it was common for a part of a community to migrate, and erect themselves into an independent society. Since the earth has been more fully peopled, and especially since the principles of Union have been better understood, a different policy has prevailed. A fondness for planting colonies has, for three preceding centuries, given full scope to a disposition for emigration, and at the same time the emigrants have been retained in a connection with their parent state. By these means Europeans have made the riches both of the east and the west subservient to their avarice and ambition. Though they occupy the smallest portion of the four quarters of the globe, they have contrived to subject the other three to their influence or command.

The circumstances under which New England was planted, would a few centuries ago have entitled them, from their first settlement, to the privileges of independence. They were virtually exiled from their native country by being denied the rights of men—they set out on their own expense, and after purchasing the consent of the

[1] David Ramsay, *The History of the American Revolution* (London, 1793), vol. 1, pp. 332–38.

native proprietors, improved an uncultivated country, to which, in the eye of reason and philosophy, the King of England had no title.

If it is lawful for individuals to relinquish their native soil, and pursue their own happiness in other regions and under other political associations, the settlers of New England were always so far independent, as to owe no obedience to their parent state, but such as resulted from their voluntary assent. The slavish doctrine of the divine right of kings, and the corruptions of Christianity, by undervaluing heathen titles to property in the soil, favored an opposite system. What for several centuries after the Christian era would have been called the institution of a new government, was by modern refinement denominated only an extension of the old, in the form of a dependent colony. Though the prevailing ecclesiastical and political creed tended to degrade the condition of the new settlers in England, yet there was always a party there which believed in their natural right to independence. They recurred to first principles, and argued, that as they received from government nothing more than a charter, founded on ideal claims of sovereignty, they owed it no other obedience than what was derived from express or implied compact. It was not till the present century had more than half elapsed, that it occurred to any number of the colonists, that they had an interest in being detached from Great Britain. Their attention was first turned to this subject by the British claim of taxation; this opened a melancholy prospect, boundless in extent. and endless in duration. The Boston port act, and the other acts, passed in 1774, and 1775, which have been already the subject of comment, progressively weakened the attachment of the colonists on the birth place of their forefathers. The commencement of hostilities on the 19th of April, 1775, exhibited the parent state in an odious point of view, and abated the original dread of separating from it. But nevertheless at that time, and for a twelve month after, a majority of the colonists wished for no more than to be re-established as subjects in their ancient rights. Had independence been their object even at the commencement of hostilities, they would have rescinded their associations which have been already mentioned, and imported goods more largely than ever. Common sense revolts at the idea, that colonists, unfurnished with military stores, and wanting manufacturers of every kind, should at the time of their intending a serious struggle for independence, by a voluntary agreement, deprive themselves of the obvious means of procuring such foreign supplies as their circumstances might make necessary. Instead of pursuing a line of conduct which might have been dictated by a wish for independence, they continued their exports for nearly a year after they ceased to import. This not only lessened the debts they owed to Great Britain, but furnished additional means for carrying on the war against themselves. To aim at independence, and at the same time to transfer their resources to their enemies, could not have been the policy of an enlightened people. It was not till some time in 1776, that the colonists began to take other ground, and contend that it was for their interest to be forever separated from Great Britain. In favor of this opinion it was said, that in case of their continuing subjects, the Mother Country, though she redressed their present grievances, might at pleasure resume similar oppressions; and that she ought not to be trusted, having twice resumed the exercise of taxation, after it had been apparently relinquished. The favorers of separation also urged, that Great Britain was jealous of their increasing numbers and rising greatness—that she would not exercise government for their benefit, but for her own. That the only permanent security for American happiness was, to deny her the power of interfering with their government or commerce. To effect this purpose they were of the opinion, that it was necessary to cut the knot which connected the two countries, by a public renunciation of all political connections between them. . . .

The favorers of subordination under the former constitution, urged the advantages of a supreme head, to control the disputes of interfering colonies, and also the benefits which flowed from union; and that independence was untried ground, and should not be entered upon but in the last extremity.

They flattered themselves that Great Britain was so fully convinced of the determined spirit of America, that if the present controversy was compromised, she would not at any future period resume an injurious exercise of her supremacy. They were therefore for proceeding no farther than to defend themselves in the character of subjects, trusting that ere long the present hostile measures would be relinquished, and the harmony of the two countries reestablished. The favorers of the system were embarrassed, and all their arguments weakened by the perseverance of Great Britain in her schemes of coercion. A probable hope of a speedy repeal of a few acts of Parliament would have greatly increased the number of those who were advocates for reconciliation. But the certainty of intelligence to the contrary gave additional force to the arguments of the opposite party. Though new weight was daily thrown into the scale, in which the advantages of independence were weighed, yet it did not preponderate till about that time in 1776, when intelligence reached the colonists of the act of Parliament passed in December 1775, for throwing them out of British protection, and of hiring foreign troops to assist in effecting their conquest. Respecting the first it was said, "that protection and allegiance were reciprocal, and that the refusal of the first was a legal ground of justification for withholding the last." They considered themselves to be thereby discharged from their allegiance, and that to declare themselves independent was no more, than to announce to the world the real political state in which Great Britain had placed them. This act proved that the colonists might constitutionally declare themselves independent, but the hiring of foreign troops to make war upon them, demonstrated the necessity of their doing it immediately. They reasoned that if Great Britain called in the aid of strangers to crush them, they must seek similar relief for their own preservation. But they well knew this could not be expected, while they were in arms against their acknowledged sovereign. They had therefore only a choice of difficulties, and must either seek foreign aid as independent states, or continue in the awkward and hazardous situation of subjects, carrying on war from their own resources, both against the King, and such mercenaries as he chose to employ for their subjugation. Necessity, not choice, forced them on the decision. Submission, without obtaining a redress of their grievances, was advocated by none who possessed the public confidence. Some of the popular leaders may have secretly wished for independence from the beginning of the controversy, but their number was small and their sentiments were not generally known.

While the public mind was balancing on this eventful subject, several writers placed the advantages of independence in various points of view. Among these Thomas Paine in a pamphlet, under the signature of Common Sense, held the most distinguished rank. The style, manner, and language of this performance were calculated to interest the passions, and to rouse all the active powers of human nature. With a view of operating on the sentiments of a religious people, Scripture was pressed into his service, and the powers, and even the name of a king was rendered odious in the eyes of the numerous colonists who had read and studied the history of the Jews, as recorded in the Old Testament. The folly of that people in revolting from a government, instituted by Heaven itself, and the oppressions to which they were subjected in consequence of their lusting after kings to rule over them, afforded an excellent handle for prepossessing the colonists in favor of republican government. Hereditary succession was turned into ridicule. The absurdity of subjecting a great continent to a small island on the other side of the globe, was represented in such striking language, as to interest the honor and pride of the colonists in renouncing the government of Great Britain. The necessity, the advantage, and practicability of independence were forcibly demonstrated. Nothing could be better timed than this performance; it was addressed to freemen, who had just received convincing proof, that Great Britain had thrown them out of her protection, had engaged foreign mercenaries to make war upon them, and seriously designed to compel their unconditional submission to her unlimited power. It found the colonists most thoroughly alarmed for their liberties, and disposed to do and suffer anything that promised their establishment. In union with the feelings and sentiments of the people, it produced surprising effects. Many thousands were convinced, and were led to approve and long for separation from the Mother Country. Though that measure, a few months before, was not only foreign from their wishes, but the object of their abhorrence, the current suddenly became so strong in its favor, that it bore down all opposition. The multitude was hurried down the stream, but some worthy men could not easily reconcile themselves to the idea of an eternal separation from a country to which they had been long bound by the most endearing ties. They saw the sword drawn, but could not tell when it would be sheathed; they feared that the dispersed individuals of the several colonies would not be brought to coalesce under an efficient government, and that after much anarchy, some future Caesar would grasp their liberties, and confirm himself in a throne of despotism. They doubted the perseverance of their countrymen in effecting their independence, and were also apprehensive that in case of success, their future condition would be less happy than their past. Some respectable individuals whose principles were pure, but whose souls were not of that firm texture which revolutions require, shrunk back from the bold measures proposed by their more adventurous countrymen. To submit without an appeal to Heaven, though secretly wished for by some, was not the avowed sentiment of any; but to persevere in petitioning and resisting, was the system of some misguided honest men. The favorers of this opinion were generally wanting in that decision which grasps at great objects, and influenced by that timid policy which does its work by halves. Most of them dreaded the power of Britain. A few, on the score of interest, or an expectancy of favors from royal government, refused to concur with the general voice. Some of the natives of the parent state, who having lately settled in the colonies, had not yet exchanged European for American ideas, together with a few others, conscientiously opposed the measures of Congress: but the great bulk of the people and especially of the spirited and independent part of the community, came with surprising unanimity into the project of independence.

The eagerness for independence resulted more from feeling than reasoning. The advantages of an unfettered trade, the prospect of honors and emoluments in administering a new government, were of themselves insufficient motives for adopting this bold measure. But what was wanting from considerations of this kind, was made up by the perseverance of Great Britain in her schemes of coercion and conquest. The determined resolution of the Mother Country to subdue the colonists, together with the plans she adopted for accomplishing that purpose, and their equally determined resolution to appeal to Heaven rather than submit, made a declaration of independence as necessary in 1776, as was the non importation agreement of 1774, or the assumption of arms in 1775. The last naturally resulted from the first. The revolution was not forced on the people by ambitious leaders grasping at supreme power, but every measure of it was forced on Congress, by the necessity of the case and the voice of the people. The change of the public mind of America respecting connections with Great Britain is without a parallel. In the short space of two years, nearly three millions of people passed over from the love and duty of loyal subjects, to the hatred and resentment of enemies.

## THOMAS JONES: A TORY VIEW OF THE REVOLUTION [2]

About the middle of June, 1776, New York being a rebel garrison in which General Washington had established his headquarters, and the Provincial Convention as well as the City Committee being then sitting, the former at the City Hall, the latter at the Exchange, a republican mob was raised in the middle of the day, headed by a number of staunch presbyterians, among whom the principal was one Lasher, a shoemaker, and then a Colonel in the rebel army, John Smith, Joshua Hett Smith, the brothers of William Smith, Esq., Peter Van Zandt, and Abraham Lott, late an alderman of the city. This mob, thus led on, searched the whole town in pursuit of tories (his Majesty's loyal subjects meaning), and found

[2] Edward Floyd De Lancey, ed., *History of New York during the Revolutionary War . . . by Thomas Jones* (New York, 1879), vol. 1, pp. 101–10.

and dragged several from their lurking holes, where they had taken refuge to avoid the undeserved vengeance of an ungovernable rabble. When they had taken several of these unhappy victims, destined to the will, the sport, and the caprice, of a banditti, and the diversion of republicans and rebels, they placed them upon sharp rails with one leg on each side; and each rail was carried upon the shoulders of two tall men, with a man on each side to keep the poor wretch straight and fixed in his seat. In this manner were numbers of these poor people, in danger of their lives from the extremity of pain occasioned by this cruel contrivance, paraded through the most public and conspicuous streets in the town, and at every corner a crier made proclamation declaring the offenders to be such and such (mentioning their names), and notorious tories (loyal subjects meaning). The mob then gave three huzzas and the procession went on. The like proclamations were made before the City Hall, where the Provincial Convention was then sitting forming laws for the civil government of the province; before the Exchange where the Committee were sitting making rules and regulations for preserving the good order, the peace and quiet of the city; and before the door of General Washington, who pretended the army under his command was raised for the defence of *American Liberty,* for the preservation of the *rights of mankind,* and for the protection of America against the unjust usurpation of the British Ministry. Notwithstanding which, so far did this humane General, and the two public bodies aforesaid, approve of this unjustifiable mob, that it received the sanction of them all. They appeared at the windows, raised their hats, returned the huzzas and joined in the acclamations of the multitude. Nay, so far did General Washington give his sanction of, and approbation to, this inhuman barbarous proceeding that he gave a very severe reprimand to General Putnam, who accidentally meeting one of the processions in the street, and shocked with its barbarity, attempted to put a stop to it, Washington declaring that to discourage such proceedings was to injure the cause of liberty in which they were then engaged, and that nobody would attempt it but an enemy to his country. Some of these unhappy victims to the vengeance of *American liberty* and the *rights of mankind* had nearly lost their lives by this fatal piece of *republican witticism.* Some were confined to their houses for many days, and not one but what received some considerable hurt from the cruel, unmerciful operation. . . .

An anecdote shall be now mentioned in order to show with how much severity the rebel chiefs were capable of treating even the wives of his Majesty's loyal subjects. A lady of the first rank, character, and family, happened to be upon a visit to some of her relations upon New York Island, attended by her postilion only, at the time that General Howe landed upon Staten Island with the army from Halifax. Upon this event General Washington issued orders that no person should pass the ferries without a written order from the commandant of the city. Not knowing who the commandant was, and the lady desirous of returning to her family upon Long Island, nearly thirty miles from the city, she wrote a polite note to General Washington begging the favor of a permit to pass the ferry. This note was delivered to General Washington by a man of character, fortune, and reputation, a near relation of the lady. Washington read the note, whispered to McDougal, turned round, tossed the paper towards the gentleman, and insultingly said, "Carry the note back to your tory relation, I have nothing to do with it, and if I had"— Here he stopped and again entered into conversation with McDougal. The gentleman however, before he returned to the lady, was informed that Lord Stirling was the commandant of the city, and that all applications for passes must be made to him. His lordship was a native of the city, was perfectly acquainted with the lady, her husband, and all their relations and connections, with some of whom he had always lived upon the terms of utmost familiarity; some favor might, therefore, be expected from him, and to him the gentleman applied. He hearkened to a relation of the particular situation in which the lady then was, and the peculiar hardships of her case, after which he sat down and deliberately wrote the following pass:

"Let Mrs. Jones pass to Long Island. *But without any male attendant.* July 4th, 1776."

"STIRLING, *Brig. General.*"

"To the Officers of the Guards."

"What!" says the gentleman, "is my cousin to mount the coach box and drive herself home?" His Lordship angrily replied, "I shall grant no other, your relation may think herself well off to have got this, and if she does not incline to make use of it, let her stay where she is *and be damned.*" She was obliged to continue several days after this, unable to return home, absent from her husband and her family, and there she might have continued until the evacuation of New York by the rebels the September following, had it not been for an honest, humane, worthy Dutchman, at that time one of the city Committee, and a member of the Provincial Convention, who being at his country seat adjoining the East River, in the neighborhood of the family where the lady then was, and hearing of her situation, was struck with astonishment. He immediately waited on her, and offered his assistance. It was gratefully accepted. He accordingly took her and her servant in a boat of his own, carried them across the river, landed them upon Long Island, and never left the lady till she entered her carriage, and the postilion drove off. The politeness and civility of this gentleman ought to be ever remembered by the lady, her friends and connections, with the utmost gratitude to the latest posterity, while the unmanly, impolite, ungenerous, and unmilitary conduct of Washington and Stirling ought to be condemned forever.

On the 30th of June, 1776, General Howe . . . landed upon Staten Island with his army from Halifax. On the 4th of July, Congress declared themselves independent States. This was followed in a very short time by a similar declaration from each colony. The General, being a joint commissioner with the Admiral, not then arrived, for restoring peace to America, attempted a negotiation with Washington, whose headquarters were in New York. Upon this subject he wrote him a letter, directed to George Washington, Esq., etc., and sent it by his adjutant-general. This letter Washington refused to receive because not directed to him as "General." General Howe, wishing for an accommodation, waived the point and directed his letter to General Washington. But he still refused to treat, insisting that no person could be authorized to negotiate in a business of this kind unless deputed by Congress, or Congress itself. The adjutant-general replied that the commissioners could not treat with Congress as a legal and constitutional body. Washington expressed great surprise. "Congress," said he, "have declared the Colonies independent of Great Britain. I am appointed by a commission from them as General of their armies. General Howe had sent him a letter directed to him as General, and his power being under Congress, the direction of that letter acknowledged the independency of the Colonies." All hope of a negotiation was now at an end. Washington transmitted the particulars to Congress, and received their thanks for his spirited conduct (as they expressed it) upon this occasion.

Washington, upon the arrival of General Howe at Staten Island, in order to prevent the people upon Long Island from either joining the royal army, supplying them with provisions, or conveying them intelligence, sent large detachments of his troops to that Island and posted them all along the shore from Yellow Hook to

Gravesend; quartered a regiment of riflemen at Rockaway; and filled the bay on the south side of the island with armed whale boats, small privateers and pettiaugers, that constantly kept patrolling the bay from Hog Island to Blue Point (distant from each other about 40 miles). Not content with this precaution, he ordered all the small craft along the shore, consisting of hay boats, canoes, batteaus, and floats, to be seized, taken away, and destroyed, or deposited in particular places under proper guards. Notwithstanding which, numbers found means to escape and join the royal army, while others, at the risk of their lives, carried them boatloads of provisions, and furnished them with all the intelligence and information necessary to be known prior to opening of the campaign.

Queen's County was extremely obnoxious to the rebels on account of the loyalty of its inhabitants, who had constantly, in spite of all oppression, ill-treatment, and hard usage, acknowledged their attachment to their sovereign; had refused to send a delegate to the Continental Congress, members to the Provincial Convention, or to elect a committee in the County. For this they were put under the ban of the 13 revolted Colonies, outlawed by an act of the Provincial Congress, not suffered to attend the New York markets, to dispose of the produce of their farms, or to prosecute, for the recovery of their just debts, while all demands against them were declared recoverable, and their property ordered, whenever found in the markets at New York, to be seized and disposed of (as pretended) for the use of the poor. Notwithstanding such pretence, many a good fat pig, a well-fed turkey, an excellent goose, or a plump dung-hill fowl, has regaled the appetite of a *rich* and *penurious* republican, forcibly taken (or rather stolen) from the Queen's County marketmen, in consequence of this act of outlawry. This was by the rebel powers called "Liberty."

Queen's County being thus obnoxious to rebellion in consequence of its firm and steady attachment to the British Constitution, and avowed opposition to all Congressional measures, a design was formed by the republicans to apprehend as many of the principal gentlemen there as possible, transport them to Connecticut, and to dragoon and compel the common people to form themselves into a militia, and join the rebel army, whenever the King's troops should land upon Long Island. To effect which a detachment of about 1,000 men, under the command of a Col. Cornell, of the Rhode Island line, by Washington's orders, marched from New York, and established his headquarters at Hempstead, nearly the centre of the County. The disaffected, consisting of about 300, out of

1,500 militia, of which the County then consisted, soon joined him. The Loyalists, having been disarmed by Hurd the preceding winter, all fled and hid themselves in swamps, in woods, in barns, in holes, in hollow trees, in corn-fields, and among the marshes. Numbers took refuge in the pine barrens in Suffolk, while others in small boats kept sailing about the Sound, landing in the night, sleeping in the woods, and taking to the water again in the morning. John Harris Cruger, Esq., one of his Majesty's Council, and Jacob Walton, Esq., one of the representatives in General Assembly, for the City of New York, were concealed for three weeks in the sultry heat of summer, upon a mow in a farmer's barn, and supplied by the owner, a loyal old Quaker, with whatever they wanted. Augustus Van Cortland, Esq., a principal gentleman, a man of family, and town clerk of the City of New York, was concealed in a cow house for a considerable time, by an honest old Dutch Loyalist, and supplied with every necessary. The rebel Colonel, having established his headquarters at Hempstead, converted the Episcopal church into a store house, forbid the parson to pray for the King or any of the Royal family, and made use of the communion table as a conveniency for his Yankees to eat their pork and molasses upon. A universal hunt after Loyalists took place, parties for that purpose were sent into every quarter of the County, under the guidance and direction of the disaffected. The Loyalists were pursued like wolves and bears, from swamp to swamp, from one hill to another, from dale to dale, and from one copse of wood to another. In consequence of which, numbers were taken, some were wounded, and a few murdered. The prisoners were conducted with infamy under a guard of rebels to New York, insulted and abused upon the road, and without a hearing, ordered by a Board of officers (appointed by Washington for that purpose) to be transported to different parts of New England. The inland parts of Connecticut became filled with loyal prisoners. The most obnoxious were imprisoned while others had the liberty of certain small districts upon parole, where they met with bad usage, rascally accommodations, and daily insults.

### HENRY C. VAN SCHAACK: PORTRAIT OF A TORY, PETER VAN SCHAACK [3]

Mr. Van Schaack was opposed to the measures of the British ministry; he anxiously desired a redress of grievances; and . . . as

[3] Henry C. Van Schaack, *The Life of Peter Van Schaack* (New York, 1842), pp. 59–62.

a member of the two committees of "fifty-one," and "sixty," he evinced his willingness to adopt measures to procure such redress. He was now solicitous to go further in the exercise of peaceful remedies; but, when it was required of him to take up arms, or to give a pledge contemplating measures of force, his conscience and his deliberate views of duty, and of the direful consequences which he apprehended would befall his country, in case of a resort to the *major vis*, would not permit him to sanction this ultimate step in the progress of the public measures. From about this period, probably, he ceased to act with the friends of the Revolution; influenced, as he evidently was, by a conviction of the great harshness in many of the public proceedings, having a direct tendency to an open rupture—by partial disgust at irregularities committed by the whigs "in the name of liberty," and by his domestic afflictions. He may be set down with probable correctness, as among that class, whom he elsewhere describes, as being "disposed to go along with the Congress to a certain limited extent, hoping in that way to fix what they conceived to be the *rights* of their country upon the firmest foundation; but as soon as they found, that the views and designs of the American leaders rested in nothing short of a dissolution of the union between Great Britain and her colonies, they refused any longer to participate in the public measures."

Having been deprived of one of the most essential organs of the human body, and with the apprehension ever present to his mind, that the secret causes which had operated to destroy the sight of one eye, might also affect the other, a new affliction awaited him, in the prospect of being deprived of the best if not his only earthly stay for consolation, should he be reduced to a state of total blindness. In August of this year, Mrs. Van Schaack was seized with a dreadful vomiting of blood, which produced a weakness in the lungs that led to a decline, which eventually terminated her life. . . .

In the midst of all these misfortunes, which seemed to "tread each other's heels," he could find no consolation in the tranquility and prosperity of his country, already distracted by the impending horrors of a civil war. The part, also, which it became *him* to take in this great contest, rendered this the most trying situation of his life. Upon mature, dispassionate and conscientious reflection, he had come to the conclusion, that it was not his duty to take up arms against the mother country. Neither did he feel himself justified in taking a part against the colonies; for, as has been seen, he condemned the prominent measures of the British government, which constituted the grievances of the colonies, and only differed with his countrymen in regard to the best remedies to be pursued.

It was not the least trying circumstances to his feelings, that in taking this position of neutrality, he found himself separated from many of the companions of his early youth, and from his most intimate friends. Not to mention others, his particular friends, John Jay, Egbert Benson, Theodore Sedgwick and Gouverneur Morris, were found among the most active advocates for warlike measures. His wishes were to have gone with these friends; his sense of duty, and of what he considered to be the best interests of the colonies, forbade his giving countenance to measures of force. The appearance of not acting up to what his best friends had rated as a standard of patriotism, and his seeming (as he supposed it would seem to others) to act against the interests of his country, gave him great pain, and operated severely upon a naturally quick sensibility, rendered particularly excitable by a series of domestic afflictions. . . .

The subject of this sketch seems to have entertained, in an eminent and peculiar degree, an abhorrence of civil war. He looked upon it as a calamity above all others to be most deprecated, and seemed scarcely willing to admit an idea of its necessity to secure a lodgment in his mind. It was his own language, upon experience, that "amidst all the calamities which are incident to mankind, those attendant upon a civil war are the most grievous, complicated, and extensive. Those who have felt its horrors, find the most animated description of them inadequate, and to those who have, by a more benign dispensation of Providence, been exempt from it, the detail of its miseries would hardly gain credit. The dissolution of the bonds of civil government, and the anarchy consequent upon it, constitute the epitome of human wretchedness."

His mind seemed to be always inclined to the dark side of the picture, and there can be no doubt, that his sentiments on this subject, in their application to the then state of public affairs, were influenced in a measure, (and probably unconsciously,) by his own personal situation. He had just commenced his professional course, which promised high distinction, and to the pursuit of which he was sincerely devoted. . . . He no doubt felt that the progress of the arts and sciences, as well as of the law, would be arrested by a state of things so uncongenial to their flourishing. The rapid succession of domestic afflictions with which he had been visited, as well as that most trying calamity which befell his eye-sight, were also calculated to predispose his mind for retirement, and for the tranquility of peace. If it be true, that character often receives its

ias from accident and situation, it will easily be perceived, that the
ircumstances referred to may have had no small share of influence
pon his mind, and the consequent government of his course.

## LORENZO SABINE: THE DIFFERENCE BETWEEN WHIG AND TORY [4]

The denial that independence was the final object, was con-
ant and general. To obtain concessions and to preserve the con-
ection with England, was affirmed everywhere; and John Adams,
ears after the peace, went further than this, for he said:—"There
as not a moment during the Revolution, when I would not have
iven everything I possessed for a restoration to the state of things
efore the contest began, provided we could have had a sufficient
ecurity for its continuance." If Mr. Adams be regarded as express-
ng the sentiments of the Whigs, *they* were willing to remain Colo-
ists, provided they could have had their rights secured to them;
hile the Tories were contented thus to continue, *without* such
ecurity. Such, as it appears to me, was the only difference between
ne two parties *prior* to hostilities; and many Whigs, like Mr. Adams,
ould have been willing to rescind the Declaration of Independ-
nce, and to forget the past, upon proper guarantees for the future.
his mode of stating the question and of defining the difference be-
ween the two parties—down to a certain period, at least—cannot
e objected to, unless the sincerity and truthfulness of some of the
nost eminent men in our history are directly impeached; and, if
ny are prepared to dispute their veracity, it may still be asked,
hether *the Tories ought not to be excused for believing* them.
ranklin's testimony *a few days before* the affair at Lexington, was,
nat he had "more than once travelled almost from one end of the
ontinent to the other, and kept a variety of company, eating, drink-
ig, and conversing with them freely, [and] never had heard in any
onversation from any person, drunk or sober, the least expression
f a wish for a separation, or a hint that such a thing would be
dvantageous to America." Mr. Jay is quite as explicit. "During
ne course of my life," said he, "and until the second petition of
Congress in 1775, I never did hear an American of any class, or of
ny description, express a wish for the independence of the Colo-
ies." "It has always been, and still is, my opinion and belief, that
ur country was prompted and impelled to independence by *neces-
ty,* and not by *choice.*" Mr. Jefferson affirmed, "What, eastward

⁴ Lorenzo Sabine, *Biographical Sketches of Loyalists of the American Revolu-
on* (Boston, 1864), vol. 1, pp. 64–68.

of New York, might have been the dispositions towards England before the commencement of hostilities, I know not; but before that I never heard a whisper of a disposition to separate from Great Britain; and after that, its possibility was contemplated with affliction by all." Washington, in 1774, fully sustains these declarations, and in the "Fairfax County Resolves" it was complained, that "malevolent falsehoods" were propagated by the ministry to prejudice the mind of the king: "Particularly that there is an intention in the American Colonies to set up for independent States." Mr. Madison was not in public life until May, 1776, but he says, "It has always been my impression, that a reestablishment of the Colonial relation to the parent country, as they were previous to the controversy, was the real object of every class of the people, till the despair of obtaining it," etc.

I have to repeat, that the only way to dispose of testimony like this is to impeach the persons who have given it. I am of Whig descent, and am proud of my lineage. With the principles of men who when it was ascertained that a redress of grievances could *not* be obtained preferred to remain British subjects, I have neither communion nor sympathy; and I may be pardoned for adding that I have watched the operations and tendencies of the Colonial system of government too long and too narrowly, modified as it now is, not to entertain for it the heartiest dislike. Yet I would do the men who were born under it, and were reconciled to it, justice—simple justice; and if as Mr. Jefferson says, a *"possibility"* of the necessity of a separation of the two countries, "was contemplated with affliction by all," and if the statements made by Franklin, Adams, Jay, Madison, and Washington, are to be considered as true and as decisive, I renewedly ask, what other line of difference existed between the Whigs and Tories, than the *terms on which the connection of the Colonies with England should be continued.*

My object in the attention bestowed on this point has been to remove the erroneous impression which seems to prevail, that the Whigs *proposed,* and the Tories *opposed* independence, at the very beginning of the controversy. . . . Quite fourteen years elapsed before the question was made a party issue, and that, even then "necessity," and not "choice," caused a dismemberment of the empire. Since it has appeared, therefore, from the highest sources, that the Whigs resolved finally upon revolution because they were denied the rights of Englishmen, and not because they disliked monarchical institutions, the Tories may be relieved from the imputation of being the only "monarchy-men" of the time. . . .

To conclude: Intelligent loyalists, when asked why they adhered to the Crown, have said, that those who received the name of "Tories" were at first, indeed for some years, striving to preserve order and an observance of the rights of persons and property; that many, who took sides at the outset as mere conservators of the peace, were denounced by those whose purposes they thwarted, and were finally compelled, in pure self-defence, to accept of royal protection, and thus to become identified with the royal party ever after. Again, it has been stated, that, had the naked question of independence been discussed before minor, and in many cases, local, events had shaped their course, many, who were driven forth to live and die as aliens and outcasts, would have terminated their career far differently; that many were opposed to war on grounds purely religious; that some thought the people enjoyed privileges enough; that others were influenced by their official connections or aspirations; that another class, who seldom mingled in the affairs of active life, loved retirement, and would, had the Whigs allowed them, have remained neutrals; that some were timid men, some were old men; and that tenants and dependents went with the landholders without inquiry, and as a thing of course. All these reasons, and numerous others, have been assigned at different times, by different persons. But another cause, quite as potent as any of these, operated, it would seem, upon thousands; namely, a dread of the strength and resources of England, and the belief that successful resistance to her power was impossible; that the Colonies had neither the men nor the means to carry on war, and would be humbled and reduced to submission with hardly an effort.

That motives and considerations, hopes and fears like these, had an influence in the formation of the *last* Colonial parties, cannot be disputed, and the unprejudiced minds of this generation should be frank enough to admit it.

## JOHN FISKE: THE TORY ISSUE IN THE PEACE SETTLEMENT [5]

The last question of all was the one most difficult to settle [in the peace negotiations]. There were many loyalists in the United States who had sacrificed everything in the support of the British cause, and it was unquestionably the duty of the British government to make every possible effort to insure them against further injury, and, if practicable, to make good their losses already incurred.

[5] John Fiske, *The Critical Period of American History, 1783–1789* (Boston, 1888), pp. 27–31.

From Virginia and the New England states, where they were few in number, they had mostly fled, and their estates had been confiscated. In New York and South Carolina, where they remained in great numbers, they were still waging a desultory war with the patriots, which far exceeded in cruelty and bitterness the struggle between the regular armies. In many cases they had, at the solicitation of the British government, joined the invading army, and been organized into companies and regiments. The regular troops defeated at King's Mountain, and those whom Arnold took with him to Virginia, were nearly all American loyalists. Lord Shelburne felt that it would be wrong to abandon these unfortunate men to the vengeance of their fellow countrymen, and he insisted that the treaty should contain an amnesty clause providing for the restoration of the Tories to their civil rights, with compensation for their confiscated property. However disagreeable such a course might seem to the victorious Americans, there were many precedents for it in European history. It had indeed come to be customary at the close of civil wars, and the effect of such a policy had invariably been good. Cromwell, in his hour of triumph inflicted no disabilities upon his political enemies; and when Charles II was restored to the throne the healing effect of the amnesty act then passed was so great that historians sometimes ask what in the world had become of that Puritan party which a moment before had seemed supreme in the land. At the close of the war of the Spanish Succession, the rebellious people of Catalonia were indemnified for their losses, at the request of England, and with a similar good effect. In view of such European precedents, Vergennes agreed with Shelburne as to the propriety of securing compensation and further immunity for the Tories in America. John Adams insinuated that the French minister took this course because he foresaw that the presence of the Tories in the United States would keep the people perpetually divided into a French party and an English party; but such a suspicion was quite uncalled for. There is no reason to suppose that in this instance Vergennes had anything at heart but the interests of humanity and justice.

On the other hand, the Americans brought forward very strong reasons why the Tories should not be indemnified by Congress. First, as Franklin urged, many of them had, by their misrepresentations to the British government, helped to stir up the disputes which led to the war; and as they had made their bed, so they must lie in it. Secondly, such of them as had been concerned in burning and plundering defenceless villages, and wielding the tomahawk in concert with bloodthirsty Indians, deserved no compassion. It was rather for them to make compensation for the misery they had wrought. Thirdly, the confiscated Tory property had passed into the hands of purchasers who had bought it in good faith and could not now be dispossessed, and in many cases it had been distributed here and there and lost sight of. An estimate of the gross amount might be made, and a corresponding sum appropriated for indemnification. But, fourthly, the country was so impoverished by the war that its own soldiers, the brave men whose heroic exertions had won the independence of the United States, were at this moment in sore distress for the want of the pay which Congress could not give them, but to which its honor was sacredly pledged. The American government was clearly bound to pay its just debts to the friends who had suffered so much in its behalf before it should proceed to entertain a chimerical scheme for satisfying its enemies. For, fifthly, any such scheme was in the present instance clearly chimerical. The acts under which Tory property had been confiscated were acts of state legislatures, and Congress had no jurisdiction over such a matter. If restitution was to be made, it must be made by the separate states. The question could not for a moment be entertained by the general government or its agents.

Upon these points the American commissioners were united and inexorable. Various suggestions were offered in vain by the British. Their troops still held the city of New York, and it was doubtful whether the Americans could hope to capture it in another campaign. It was urged that England might fairly claim in exchange for New York a round sum of money wherewith the Tories might be indemnified. It was further urged that certain unappropriated lands in the Mississippi valley might be sold for the same purpose. But the Americans would not hear of buying one of their own cities, whose independence was already acknowledged by the first article of the treaty which recognized the independence of the United States; and as for the western lands, they were wanted as a means of paying our own war debts and providing for our veteran soldiers. Several times Shelburne sent word to Paris that he would break off the negotiation unless the loyalist claims were in some way recognized. But the Americans were obdurate. They had one advantage, and knew it. Parliament was soon to meet, and it was doubtful whether Lord Shelburne could command a sufficient majority to remain long in office. He was, accordingly, very anxious to complete the treaty of peace, or at least to detach America from the French Alliance, as soon as possible. The American commissioners were also eager to conclude the treaty. They had secured very favorable terms, and were loath to run any risk of spoiling what had been done. Accordingly, they made a proposal in the form of a compromise, which nevertheless settled the point in their favor. The matter, they said, was beyond the jurisdiction of Congress, but they agreed that Congress should *recommend* to the several states to desist from further proceedings against the Tories, and to reconsider their laws on this subject; it should further recommend that persons with claims upon confiscated lands might be authorized to use legal means of recovering them, and to this end might be allowed to pass to and fro without personal risk for the term of one year. The British commissioners accepted this compromise, unsatisfactory as it was, because it was really impossible to obtain anything better without throwing the whole negotiation overboard.

### LEONARD W. LABAREE: THE TORY MIND [6]

There were individual and group differences among the Loyalists and, for many of them, such as officeholders, owners of large property, and merchants, questions of economic self-interest played a significant part. Having first recognized these facts, we must understand the following eight points if we are to understand the men who finally sided with the British in the great dispute: First, they were men of an essentially conservative temperament, disposed from the start to resist innovation and to support the old and the familiar. Second, many though not all of them held the conviction, based usually on religious belief and church affiliation, that, whatever the merits of the dispute, resistance to constituted authority and to the British government was morally wrong. Third, while a few sided with the ministry from the beginning, most Loyalists reached their final position only slowly and after much difficulty. One of the major factors that led many of them to make this decision was that they were alienated from the supporters of resistance by the continued use of violence and other forms of extreme action. Fourth, some men were really forced into out-and-out loyalism by the refusal of their fellow colonists to permit them to keep to a middle-of-the-road position. Fifth, there was a sentimental attachment to Britain, an admiration for the constitution, and a belief in the value of the British connection, all of which made men reluctant to

[6] Leonard W. Labaree, *Conservatism in Early American History* (New York: New York University Press, 1948), pp. 164–66. © 1948 by New York University. Reprinted with the permission of the publisher.

break with the mother country. Sixth, we can recognize the very human tendency to procrastinate. While many conservatives admitted that eventually independence woul' ~~ inevitable, they wanted to put off the evil day and so refused *Toru* it the time for such action had now arrived. Seventh, th d was cautious. Men were reluctant to accept an un re without guarantees that it would provide conditions _ satisfactory as those they were giving up. Eighth and last, the Loyalist was pessimistic. He feared that the disturbed conditions of the Revolutionary period would be perpetuated if America gained her independence and that the new regime would raise the ignorant, disorderly element of society to a position of permanent and undesirable supremacy. He had little faith in the political capacity of the average American. These, I believe, were the essential features of Tory thinking. They all represent typically conservative attitudes. In displaying these characteristics during the great crisis the American Loyalist earned the right to be considered the culminating example of the colonial conservative.

Participation in revolution—except for those whose motives are most narrowly selfish—requires a special kind of imaginative courage, one compounded of a general bravery in the face of an uncertain future, faith in that future, a power to imagine vividly how it may be molded to a desired end, and an optimistic disregard of the possibilities of loss or of failure to attain the hoped-for goal. All great revolutionaries have had that sort of courage, whether or not the movements they led have, in the long perspective of history, been successful, or have sought ends to the real interest of humanity. The conservatives who have opposed such revolutions—again apart from those whose motives have been primarily ones of self-interest—have seldom been endowed with this sort of courage. Again and again they have displayed a different group of virtues: a strong sense of the values in the contemporary order of society that are in danger of being lost, an imagination keen enough to see the possible harm as well as the good in the changes proposed, and a personal bravery in the face of suffering and persecution.

Thus it was with the sincere Loyalists of the American Revolution. They saw more clearly than did some of their opponents the values inherent in their colonial past, in the tradition of government by law which was theirs under the British constitution, and in the strength and external security afforded by the British connection. They recognized the dangers threatening a future state founded in violence and disorder by a group of leaders many of whom were quite inexperienced in the art of government. And when their turn came to suffer in their persons and in their property and even by banishment or death, many of the Loyalists made the required sacrifice with a dignity and fortitude worthy of the highest admiration. What they lacked, what made them Loyalists rather than revolutionists, was the other sort of courage and imagination. They saw the dangers ahead rather than the noble possibilities. They did not have the daring needed to strike for a better future even at the risk of losing a present good. They lacked—many of them—a sufficient faith in mankind, in common, American mankind, to believe that out of disorder and violence, out of an inexperienced leadership and an undisciplined following, could come a stable and intelligent body politic. They were Loyalists, in short, because they had both the weakness and the strength of all true conservatives.

## PAUL H. SMITH: ENGLAND'S MILITARY USE OF THE TORIES [7]

While Loyalists took a leading role in the pre-Revolutionary debates, urging caution, suggesting compromise, and defeating extreme solutions, they quickly withdrew to the sidelines when the struggle settled down to a test of arms. Consequently, although a significant minority immediately took the initiative and plotted their own independent courses of action—in much the same manner as the most determined revolutionists—most Loyalists patiently awaited Britain's guidance and leadership.

It was precisely this situation that Britain failed to grasp; unaware of the possibilities of Loyalist support, government only half-heartedly asserted that leadership in the early months of the contest. Of the many mistakes Britain made with her American colonies, none was more costly or had more far-reaching consequences than her assumption that numerous Loyalists would without encouragement continue after 1775 to accept responsibilities as they had during the preceding decade. The error was easily made and difficult to correct; it followed readily from several basic British beliefs. Most Englishmen believed the majority of Americans to be essentially loyal, the bulk of the rebels too cowardly and poorly trained to face the British army, and Loyalists resolutely determined to prevent the overthrow of imperial authority. Before 1778, the

[7] Paul H. Smith, *Loyalists and Redcoats*, Institute of Early American History and Culture (Williamsburg, Virginia: University of North Carolina Press, 1964), pp. 168–74. Reprinted with the permission of the publisher.

Loyalists' assistance was simply presumed to be unneeded. Thus without seeking to determine the precise contribution they might make, government from the outset failed to make adequate preparations to organize them effectively.

Surprisingly, this initial failure in no way weakened government's confidence in the ultimate usefulness and dependability of the Loyalists. Indeed, during the first two years of the war, when little official effort was directed to mobilizing Loyalists, their eagerness to form provincial corps and participation in a few hastily conceived Loyalist projects strengthened that confidence. What officials failed to perceive, however, was that this response was not merely the result of Loyalist zeal of British plans but largely of conditions which were unlikely to persist. Loyalists at this time acted not because of, but in absence of, positive encouragement. The initiative in every case came from America, not London. Their motives were conditioned by fear of rebel reprisals, proximity of the British army, and a presumption that the war would be of brief duration. Britain's policy was as yet inchoate, consisting of little more than a few regulations to govern the first Loyalists who early forced their unwanted attentions upon the administration. It was impossible from their initial response to assume that mere policy changes and more liberal inducements would readily elicit decisive Loyalist participation.

The ambivalence of Britain's early Loyalist policy—which coupled reluctance to organize them with surpassing confidence in their usefulness—made the administration's subsequent plans appear contradictory. Furthermore, in light of her meager efforts to mobilize Loyalists before 1778, Britain's paralyzing dependence upon them in later stages of the war appears incomprehensible. Careful examination easily resolves the confusion. British overconfidence, the tendency to underestimate the enemy, and the North ministry's reluctance to expand the Provincial Service, which marked British policy during Howe's command, no longer crippled British planning after 1778. Saratoga and the French entry combined to destroy government's propensity to employ half-measures against the revolutionists. Thus, Britain subsequently turned to every resource at her command and eagerly sought aid from every feasible quarter, which included above all cooperation of the American Loyalists. . . .

Just as the prospect of Loyalist support decisively shaped over-all policy, so too did that anticipated support mold actual southern operations. Indeed, after 1779, continuation of the war against the colonies depended upon the cooperation of Loyalists in re-establishing royal government in the South. Although decisive victory at Charleston appeared to destroy opposition in South Carolina, Cornwallis nevertheless soon found that Britain's loyalist plans were in peril. Marching into the interior in August to bolster the loyalist experiment, Cornwallis administered a second crushing defeat to the Americans, but the victory failed to put him nearer his original goal. Because the situation in the South rested heavily upon Loyalist support, victory in the field alone was never sufficient to insure permanent success. By September, the Loyalists were in control of very little territory outside the immediate vicinity of Charleston, and the backcountry was aflame with revolt. Thus in October Cornwallis started northward to rally the North Carolina Loyalists and to cut off all outside support for the South Carolina revolutionists, but the incredible rebel victory at King's Mountain disrupted his march.

Before Cornwallis resumed the campaign, the situation in the South had changed completely. The destruction of Loyalists under Major Ferguson at King's Mountain and arrival of another American army in the South under General Greene practically destroyed all prospects of organizing the Carolina Loyalists. Sensing this fact, Cornwallis readied his troops for another North Carolina campaign, which, in cooperation with a newly arrived expedition in the Chesapeake, might enable him completely to clear the southern colonies of armed rebels. When a second disaster befell him at the Cowpens before he was fairly under way, however, his operations temporarily lost all sense of direction. Blindly striking out after Morgan and Greene—a maneuver which lost him both his baggage train and the crucial race to the Dan—Cornwallis in February suddenly found himself several hundred miles from his nearest support and totally unequipped to complete his original plans with the North Carolina Loyalists. Although he paid lip service to this project during the following weeks, he gradually abandoned the Loyalist experiment—and with it the primary purpose of the southern campaign. A bloody engagement with Greene at Guilford Courthouse failed to improve his position. Seemingly unaware that his army's condition and the presence of Greene's troops rendered it unlikely that Loyalists would now foolhardily expose themselves, he nevertheless once again called them to the royal standard. Upon encountering a very meager response he precipitately abandoned the Carolinas to Greene, convinced that any campaign dependent upon cooperation from the Loyalists was completely unsound. . . .

Government proposed no fundamental strategic changes after 1780. Unable to acquire new support in Parliament, the ministry refused to hazard its precarious position by altering basic designs in America. Laboring under severe censure, at war with powerful European enemies, and beset by financial woes, government doggedly clung to the hope that Loyalists might yet rally vigorously and thereby convince the revolutionists of the futility of remaining in rebellion. In light of the ministry's plight, no other course was open.

Eventually, that cherished hope proved wholly illusory; even before Cornwallis surrendered at Yorktown the fantasy of the belief had become apparent. In America, Clinton was unable to produce permanent results with the set strategy, but as commander in chief he accepted his responsibility to make the attempt. Learning that no new reinforcements would be sent from Europe, he made the best of an impossible task; although he expressed reservations about government's Loyalist plans, he continued preparations to put them into effect in the only areas which remained untested. The breakdown of communications between Clinton and Cornwallis during the summer of 1781 frustrated even these efforts. Accordingly, when Cornwallis's army was captured in Virginia, a majority in the Commons refused to support continuation of the war on such a sterile basis as Loyalist cooperation.

In dealing with the Loyalists, Britain made two palpable errors: she turned to them for assistance much too late, and then relied upon them much too completely. Basic ignorance of colonial conditions and sheer incompetence, to be sure, lay at the core of these errors. Equally, however, they were committed because government was not at any time entirely at liberty to conduct the war on purely military grounds. Thus foreign intervention, political pressures, and poor intelligence led to adoption of a policy which had major limitations at best and grave defects at worst. Never free to wage total war in America, Britain inaccurately gauged the possibilities and limitations of the restricted warfare which alone she was free to pursue. Only vaguely aware of these subtle limitations, she relied upon a series of inconsistent plans, of which her Loyalist policy was the least well managed. That confused policy stands as a monument to the hazards which inhere in the conduct of limited war.

## WALLACE BROWN: KEYS TO UNDERSTANDING LOYALISM [8]

No one who studies the Loyalists for any length of time can doubt that among the educated a genuine, often touching, zeal for the British constitution flourished. This very rarely meant approval of the unpopular parliamentary legislation since 1763; but it did mean trust in the basic system and in peaceful methods of redress. Also, such loyalists pointed to the amazing growth and prosperity of the colonies within the empire and to the great freedom already enjoyed; how much more could a reasonable man want, they asked, and many argued that if anything the power of the masses should be diminished.

But comparatively few Loyalists took a reasoned position. Most colonists, like most people anywhere, followed their leaders. Thus the quality and type of leaders, Whig and Tory, is important. This helps to explain why Loyalism barely existed in Virginia and was strong in South Carolina, why it was stronger in New York than in Massachusetts.

Self-interest and greed are obviously important factors in all human affairs and Loyalism is no exception. Many examples in various colonies have been given of merchants who traded with the British during the war, a fact which probably induced loyalty. James Simpson reported to the claims commissioners: "Such were the incidents of the war, that the profits upon a single voyage sometimes enabled the Adventurers, not only to emerge from indigence and obscurity, but to rise to a great degree of opulence. . . ." However, the Whig side was often economically more attractive. Schlesinger has suggested that although the merchants did not usually favor independence, "the line of least resistance" was to accept it, especially if their wealth was not removable, and their business and customers could not be transferred to the British lines. Also, although many lawyers were Loyalists, many others, like certain merchants, were sham Whigs. William Franklin reported that Isaac Ogden, a New Jersey lawyer who was a member of the provincial congress, went in "as many of his profession did, with a view of promoting his popularity and preventing others from running away with his business." Hard money was often a tempta-

[8] Wallace Brown, *The King's Friends: The Composition and Motives of the American Loyalist Claimants* (Providence, Rhode Island: Brown University Press, 1965), pp. 278–83. © 1965 by Brown University. Reprinted with permission of the publisher.

tion over paper continentals. When the British troops returned to Charleston, Joshua Lockwood, a substantial mechanic, changed from Whiggery to Toryism in order to collect his debts in specie.

Whether it was true or not, several Tories (especially in Boston) from split families were suspected of opportunism, of deliberately splitting so that the family would retain the property whichever side won. Benjamin Pickman fled from Salem, Massachusetts, in 1775, but left his wife behind to look after their property, to which he returned ten years later. The Dulanys of Maryland were charged with a similar subterfuge.

Similarly, quite apart from the consideration of their oaths, royal and proprietary officials would lose their jobs by rebellion. But even if they never guessed that they would lose them, many office-holders were able people who could have had, and indeed frequently were offered, attractive appointments with the Whig regimes. Thus, loyalty was certainly not always a simple case of self-interest, a conclusion reinforced by the number of merchant partners who chose opposite sides (assuming the economic interest was clear).

Thomas McKean's identification of the Loyalists with the "timid" has sometimes been taken up by historians, and other contemporaries agreed with the Pennsylvania statesman. Ambrose Serle, who as secretary to Lord Howe in New York became disillusioned with the Loyalists, in December, 1776, quoted his master as observing "to me this morning, that almost all the people of parts and spirit were in rebellion." A few days later Serle himself complained of the Loyalists, "alas, they all prate and profess much; but when you call upon them, they will *do* nothing." Lord Cornwallis also designated the Loyalists as "timid," and while praising their fortitude condemned their "indecision."

Perhaps most men of "parts" were Patriots; the Loyalist leadership could not remotely match the Whig in talent. Some Loyalists were undoubtedly timid. (This especially the case in South Carolina.) They were afraid of the turbulence and change of the Revolution—Crévecôeur was held back by the "respect I feel for the ancient connection, and the fear of innovations, with the consequences of which I am not well acquainted"—and convinced that the British army, the representative, after all, of the greatest empire the world had yet seen, must triumph. They shared Samuel Curwen's strong conviction of the almost physical impossibility of the colonies' "waging a successful war" with Great Britain.

But timidity was not always, or perhaps even usually, the rule.

Some Loyalists were never daunted, such as Philip Skene, of Skenes-borough, New York, who, Governor Franklin related, even when jailed at Hartford, Connecticut, would "still harangue the people from the prison windows." Joshua North of Delaware was so anxious to join the British army in 1779 in Carolina that he rode the 1,100 miles, 400 of which were under snow, and often slept in "a temporary hut of Saplins."

It took great courage to express a violently unpopular minority view, to undergo social ostracism, economic ruin, and even physical torture and death, which many suffered with great fortitude. Admittedly these were not normally the results that had been expected, but many Loyalists stuck to their position even when it was clear they were on the losing side. The claims commission testimony is replete with examples of Loyalists who refused tempting offers of official positions with the rebels. Further, many Loyalists were so in spite of the lack of British encouragement and even in the face of British harassment, complaints of which are a common feature of the claims commission testimony and of Loyalist writings.

Other keys to Loyalism than timidity have been offered. William H. Nelson has suggested that the various Loyalist groups were usually "cultural minorities" in need of British help or protection and fearful of an increase in the power of the majority.

This view is echoed by William W. Sweet who rightly points out that the number of Anglican Loyalists is in inverse proportion to the strength of the church; thus in New England they were loyal almost to a man, in Virginia most Anglicans were Whig. . . .

Most Loyalists had, or thought they had, something material or spiritual to lose from the break with Britain. This fear was the great unifying factor. Officials had their jobs to lose, lawyers their fees, merchants their trade, landowners their proprietorships, Anglicans their dream of a bishop, king-worshippers and aristocrats their idol, Anglophiles their membership in the empire, some Regulators and Massachusetts Baptists their hope of royal help, Negroes their freedom, Indians the British alliance against the frontiersman. Conservatives and the better off in general had most to lose in a revolutionary upheaval; the timid became Loyalists in areas occupied by British troops; some officeholders, and perhaps the Highlanders were loath to break their oaths of allegiance.

John Eardly-Wilmot, one of the claims commissioners, began his inquiry with no particular liking for the Loyalists, but long familiarity with their misfortune produced in him considerable admiration, so that his account of the claims commission proceedings, published in 1815, was prefaced, rather appropriately, with the following lines from Milton:

> Their Loyalty they kept, their love, their zeal,
> Nor number, nor example with them wrought
> To swerve from truth, or change their constant mind.

## WILLIAM A. BENTON: THE WHIG-LOYALISTS [9]

The Whig-Loyalists functioned as Patriots before the American Revolution and then became supporters of British rule in America. Seemingly, they changed sides, broke with their old allegiance, and joined the very faction and power they had been fighting. The key to understanding these men is the fact that they were members of the upper and upper middle classes of colonial society. They were oligarchs and functioned as they did for logical reasons. The Whig-Loyalists adhered to conservative Whig principles—principles which upheld oligarchy. Therefore, their behavior can only be understood if one accepts the existence of an oligarchical pattern in American colonial politics.

The American Revolution was more than a war for independence and more than a civil war between two conflicting political ideologies—Whiggery and Toryism. It was also a struggle between two oligarchies in each of the colonies. By and large the colonial governments were controlled by an oligarchy consisting of the upper social and economic class. Almost all of the political leaders of the revolutionary period were members of an oligarchy in their respective colonies. Whether they were Patriots or Tories they had that in common.

The Whig and Tory oligarchies were essentially identical in their functions, behavior and makeup. Composed of the social and economic elite of the colonies, these groups made policy and provided continuity for their respective political movements. Both attempted to seize and hold the reins of government in order to perpetuate the power of the oligarchy. However, the basis of their power did differ. To some extent the Whig oligarchs supported and worked through the colonial assemblies. They attempted to gain power and perpetuate their own rule by making the assembly the center of power and patronage in the colony, with themselves functioning

[9] William A. Benton, *Whig-Loyalism: An Aspect of Political Ideology in the American Revolutionary Era* (Rutherford, New Jersey: Associated University Press, Inc., 1969), pp. 14–18. Reprinted with the permission of the publisher.

as leaders of the legislature. Since the power of the Whig oligarchy was centered in the assembly it had some degree of popular support. This support was necessary to the existence of the oligarchy since the so-called mechanic and small farmer in America did possess important political rights. But that is not to say that politics in the American colonies were in any sense egalitarian. Although dependent upon the support of the common man, the Whig oligarchy was safeguarded by property qualifications for the participation in government and by the overrepresentation of the eastern, more settled sections of the colony.

The oligarchies which were later to be stigmatized with the epithet "Tory" attempted to maintain a position of power by controlling the governorship and the council, although the council control was contested by the Whigs in many colonies. In most respects the Tories were distrustful of representative institutions and tried to maintain their power by keeping the reins of power and patronage in the hands of the royal governor. They then hoped to be able to control this instrument of royal authority in the colonies. This stand, of necessity, meant that during the revolutionary era they supported the efforts of Parliament to centralize authority in the empire and opposed all conceptions of legislative privilege for the colonial assemblies.

It is understandable that, in some respects, historians have tended to portray the American Revolution as an intense struggle between two neatly defined parties, the Whigs and the Tories. This tidy picture of a struggle between two ideologies tends to simplify any study of the period. But in order to undertake an objective study of the Whig-Loyalists, one must reject this polarization and all sharply defined patterns of mass behavior. For the Whig-Loyalist, in essence, did not conform to the ideological pattern of either the Whig or Tory grouping.

While the Revolution did not pit neatly polarized groups of Whigs and Tories against each other, the Whig-Loyalists were not the only group to behave in what appeared to be an ambivalent fashion during these critical years. Indecision and ambivalence were important and complex factors during the revolutionary era. Several kinds of ambivalence and indecision existed in between the normal polarities of Whig and Tory, of which Whig-Loyalism is only one, albeit an extremely important one. Besides Whig-Loyalism, at least six other categories of belief and conduct that fall between the extremes of Whiggery and Toryism can be described.

Firstly, there were religious neutrals, such as Moses Brown of Providence and other Quakers, who supported the Whig cause but who could not participate in the War for Independence. They were, therefore, neither active Patriots nor Loyalists. Secondly, there were men such as Rev. William Smith, provost of the College of Philadelphia, who cautiously endorsed colonial resistance, then opposed it, but did not become an overt Loyalist. Third, there was a whole category of clergymen described . . . as rationalists. These men were alienated from the Revolution by its Calvinist leadership and were either reluctant Patriots, outright Loyalists, or covert opponents of the Revolution. Fourth, there were men such as Governor William Franklin of New Jersey and Lieutenant Governor William Bull of South Carolina, American-born crown officials who sympathized to some degree with Whig principles but nonetheless remained loyal to Great Britain. Fifth, there were neutralists like Robert Beverley of Virginia who mildly supported the Whig position during the Stamp Act crisis. They later became disenchanted with the revolutionary movement and were able to remain neutralists during the war. And last, there were men who did not openly support colonial resistance but privately sympathized with it and later became Loyalists. These men were, in effect, passive Whig-Loyalists.

Substantial differences exist between these six categories of ambivalence and the Whig-Loyalists. While these six groups of men were irresolute, the Whig-Loyalists were neither ambivalent nor indecisive. During the course of the revolutionary struggle they made decisive changes of affiliation in keeping with their ideological beliefs. During the early years of the struggle for colonial rights the Whig-Loyalists upheld the prevailing colonial notions of legislative independence. They were active Patriots during the agitation over the Stamp Act and resisted the Tory effort to centralize the empire. When open revolt began in April, 1775 the Whig-Loyalists in most cases advocated the use of armed force to gain autonomy for the colonies. But when forced to decide upon the question of independence, their fear of social upheaval and their devotion to conservative Whiggery kept all of them loyal to the empire.

The Whig-Loyalists did not become Tories in 1776. They continued to distinguish themselves from the Tories during and after the war. Thus they did not conform to the ideological pattern of either Whigs or Tories. By studying the Whig-Loyalists, one can see the danger of polarizing all Americans in the revolutionary era into two neat groups. One can also better understand the large element of conservatism in the philosophy of the American Whigs, as well as the strength of American attachment to the British empire.

## L. F. S. UPTON: THE REWARDS OF LOYALTY— THE CASE OF WILLIAM SMITH [10]

Born in dissent, buried in the Church of England: a fitting epitaph for many a successful man, consistent with the rise from political agitator to office-holder. It is hardly surprising that [William] Smith's descendants were staunch supporters of the Anglican church. Yet he himself never made that transition, never tied the numerous strands of his life into one convenient knot.

It would be simple to present Smith as a politician with his eye on the main chance, using his considerable legal skills to advance himself. Learning both his profession and his politics from his father, he fought the New York De Lanceys who had excluded his family from influence. He began his career as a devotee of the "whig" cause; yet his ardor soon cooled, for at the very time he acquired the nickname "Patriotic Billy" he was doubting the wisdom of a political course that urged men dangerously towards violence. A successful legal practice and increasing investment in land made Smith wary; appointment to the royal Council bespoke a stake in society that should not be jeopardized. From then on his career was set: office-holding led to loyalty during the American Revolution, loyalty to ever greater rewards, culminating in appointment as chief justice of Quebec.

Another straightforward view of Smith's career would be to interpret his every move in the light of a determination to hold on to his investments at all costs. It was a remarkable achievement to be one of the three Loyalists whose property was not confiscated by the state of New York; even more remarkable to be a New Yorker Loyalist and still retain lands in Vermont. It could be argued that the protection of his lands dictated his political course from the governorship of Lord Dunmore onward; that Smith sat out the early years of the war expecting a quick British victory; that he betrayed the secret negotiations with Vermont to curry favor

[10] L. F. S. Upton, *The Loyal Whig: William Smith of New York and Quebec* (Toronto: University of Toronto Press, 1969), pp. 218–21. © 1969 by the University of Toronto Press. Reprinted with the permission of the publisher.

with the revolutionaries of New York; that he favored a special relationship between post-war Quebec and Vermont to guarantee his property in that independent little republic. But such an approach can be only a partial explanation, an examination of one stratum of Smith's activities.

What complicates any summation of Smith's political career is the fact that he never ceased being a dissenter. He was forever fighting an establishment, even when he was obviously part of it. He spoke often of the need for balance in political society, for monarchy, aristocracy, as well as democracy. Yet in his New York the balance was always out of kilter, and he always felt it necessary to overemphasize democracy to re-establish equilibrium. He always saw an immediate purpose in calling on the democratic element to agitate. The results were relatively harmless as long as the bounds were finite and within the context of the British American political society he knew. As he grew older and wealthier this dissent also had the virtue of presenting him with a choice: to acknowledge his acquired position as a conservative, or to rely on his past as a "popular" politician. Smith had no intention of giving up the luxury of choice.

With the drift into rebellion, the consequences of agitation became infinite. Yet Smith still avoided decisive action. He retired to think matters over, although thought alone produced no resolve. By avoiding public life he hoped to keep his options open. In his own mind even his joining the British in 1778 was something less than a final choice. Appointed chief justice and once more an active member of the royal Council, he naturally found those in office incompetent; but now that he was in public life again too much activity would bring too much prominence which in turn would imperil his freedom of action. He was not disturbed when the state of New York banished him, for his lands were not confiscated. Reading between the lines he could take comfort in the thought that he still had the alternative of returning to his past. Even in London he clung to the hope that he could go home if the British government failed to meet his just demands. Not until 1785 did Smith realize that he had run out of alternatives, and that the only hope left lay in the patronage of Sir Guy Carleton. . . .

William Smith the politician is a fascinating study of a man of uncertain motives who documented his own weaknesses in great detail. He revealed the hesitations, suspicions, self-deceptions, and special pleadings that have determined the careers of more men than would ever confess to such defects. These deficiencies explain why Smith left no great accomplishments behind him as a politician, but they make his career a valuable commentary on the great events of his time.

A skirmisher in practical politics, Smith was a veritable supreme commander when it came to theory. Here equivocation gave way to certainty, and the destiny of peoples was arranged with unfailing decision. In publishing his *History* he showed an early and keen appreciation of the fact that New York was but one part of a great empire. This was an unusual quality among colonial politicians who lived in societies as egocentric as those of Greek city states. Smith had a continuous regard for the empire as a unit, beneficial to all its partners. At the time of the Stamp Act crisis he led moderate and successful opposition to Parliament, but recognized the significance of victory. Parliament had been forced to repeal legislation imposing a tax on the colonies. If another conflict were to arise, would the distinction between taxing and lawmaking survive? Smith's plans for an American parliament aimed at drawing a distinct line between the two powers in order to end the confusion.

When the American Revolution broke out, Smith maintained the distinction clearly before his eyes: Parliament had no right to tax the colonies; the colonies had no right to reject the legislative supremacy of Parliament. Resistance to parliamentary taxation was justifiable but independence was not. It was an obvious distinction to make, but one which most of his contemporaries on both sides of the Atlantic could not, or would not, see. The House of Commons contributed to the confusion by insisting on its power to tax. Many prominent Englishmen, among them successive military commanders, opposed the idea of taxing the colonies and were therefore inclined to sympathize with the revolutionaries.

Smith's great hope was to be able to cut through this confusion of thought, and to separate, in the minds of men, these two distinct powers. Give the Americans a continental assembly to enable them to tax themselves for the benefit of the empire, he said. From the first he considered Congress a body competent to treat with Britain; Americans normally summoned a congress in times of crisis and it did not appear to him to be an assembly of rebels with no legal standing. As the colonies muddled into war with the mother country, Smith maintained a distinction between powers that was ceasing to have any relevance to the situation. As the war lengthened, he maintained his conviction of the iniquity of parliamentary taxation at the same time as he believed independence to be impossible.

The Revolution could only bring death and destruction to his native land, and he wanted a swift end to the war, favoring strong British measures, as a man cauterizes a wound that in one sharp agony he may purge himself of a mortal infection.

# Afterword

Is loyalty an allegiance to the ideals of a nation? If so, the rebels remained loyal: their aim was to keep intact the essence of what was best in their heritage. Is loyalty an allegiance to a nation, whether its policies uphold its ideals? If so, the Tories remained loyal: patriotism above idealism was the first necessity. Love of one's country could be polarized into two opposite camps. Either one loved the concepts upon which that nation was founded, or one loved the nation as it was, not ideally but concretely. To the Tories, the nation as it stood was more important than the ideals it originally had stood upon. And yet if loyalty is, as Henry Steele Commager describes it, "a tradition, an ideal, and a principle" the rebels held on to the best and discarded the rest. And if it is, as Commager says, "a willingness to subordinate every private advantage for larger good," the Tories were more loyal to themselves than to their fellow man.

The questions which divided Whig and Tory are as old as western culture. Is it better to endure or disrupt? At what point does too much order become despotism? Too much liberty become anarchy? At what point is revolt—with all its attendant violence and bloodshed—justified by circumstances? Or is revolt too radical a surgery, never to be justified? Thomas Jefferson believed that mankind had always differed over these questions. "In fact," he noted in a letter to John Adams in 1813, "the terms whig and tory belong to natural, as well as to civil history. They denote the temper and constitution of mind of different individuals."

To be sure, Jefferson could scarcely envision the sophisticated issues of the twentieth century. Industrialism and imperialism have multiplied problems and complicated solutions. The Marxist strategy of class revolt and the concept of a dictatorship of the proletariat are grounded in a philosophy radically different from eighteenth-century natural-law theories upon which Jefferson built his rationalization of revolution. Nevertheless, the idea of characterizing individuals into two types—whig and tory—is still valid. Leonard Labaree has described the rebel type in universal terms. "Participation in revolution," he writes, "except for those whose motives are most narrowly selfish, requires a special kind of imaginative courage, one compounded of a general bravery in the face of an uncertain future, faith in that future, a power to imagine vividly how it may be molded to a desired end, and an optimistic disregard of the possibilities of loss or of failure to attain the hoped-for goal." The Tory lacked this kind of optimistic daring. He believed that rebel dissent was irresponsible; protesting specific evils did not justify greater misdeeds; to subject a people to the turmoil of war, the loss of life, and the expense of arms was a far greater wrong than any offense the British government had committed. To subject a people to all this, simply for the promise of better days—an illusion, a boast, but certainly not a definite reality—was worse than any tangible malignancy.

Perhaps people shall always disagree about political systems—one group exalting the past, eschewing violence, retaining hope of reform from within, believing that people can ever progress by peaceful means; the other group believing that governments controlled by a favorite few, and grown hoary with corruption, are better destroyed and reconstituted upon more democratic principles. The United States was the first nation to be so created. But in the twentieth century, one wonders whether its ideals have been fulfilled or perverted; one wonders whether vital social reforms can be accomplished from within.

# Bibliographical Note

The American Tories—at least those of the intellectual elite—were understandably articulate in expressing their philosophy, their motives, and their experiences. Many were American-born and, if loyal to England, they still missed their native land. As expatriates they congregated in the London coffee-houses, tragic figures seeking solace in each other's company. Some remained to die in exile; some drifted back to the United States in later years. Quite a few recorded their personal stories, and the best introduction to the subject of the American Tory is their own letters, journals, and reminiscences. The following seven works are particularly recommended: Samuel Curwen, *The Journal and Letters of Samuel Curwen* (Boston, 1864); John W. Lydekker, *The Life and Letters of Charles Inglis* (London, 1936); Henry C. Van Schaack, *The Life of Peter Van Schaack* (New York, 1842); Clarence H. Vance, ed., *Letters of a Westchester Farmer by Reverend Samuel Seabury* (White Plains, New York, 1930); Douglass Adair and John C. Shutz, eds., *Peter Oliver's Origin and Progress of the American Revolution* (Stanford, 1961); Jonathan Boucher, *Reminiscences of an American Loyalist* (Boston, 1925); Thomas Hutchinson, *Diary and Letters of Thomas Hutchinson* (Boston, 1884–86), 2 volumes. There are also several well edited collections of sources that contain selections of loyalist material. Especially noteworthy are those by L. F. S. Upton, ed., *Revolutionary Versus Loyalist* (Waltham, Massachusetts, 1968) and G. N. D. Evans, ed., *Allegiance in America: The Case of the Loyalists* (Reading, Massachusetts, 1969). A superbly edited collection, covering the entire range of the American Revolution, is *The Spirit of 'Seventy-Six* (Indianapolis, 1958), 2 volumes, edited by Henry Steele Commager and Richard B. Morris.

Histories of the loyalists in particular states vary considerably in quality. As a general rule older works tend to be more descriptive and narrative than interpretive. Nevertheless, they contain material of great value and one can profit from a reading of any of the following: Alexander C. Flick, *Loyalism in New York during the American Revolution* (New York, 1901); Otis G. Hammond, *Tories of New Hampshire in the War of the Revolution* (Concord, New Hampshire, 1917); James H. Stark, *The Loyalists of Massachuestts* (Boston, 1910); Harold B. Hancock, *The Delaware Loyalists* (Bloomington, Delaware, 1940); Robert O. DeMond, *The Loyalists in North Carolina during the Revolution* (Durham, North Carolina, 1940). DeMond's attempt to link the Regulator movement with the loyalists has been rebutted by Hugh T. Lefler and Albert R. Newsome in *North Carolina: The History of a Southern State* (Chapel Hill, 1954). A modern study of the Regulators by Richard M. Brown, *The South Carolina Regulators* (Cambridge, 1963), also denies the thesis of a connection between the Regulators and the loyalists. For Maryland the finest study of loyalism is in the form of a family biography by Aubrey C. Land, *The Dulanys of Maryland* (Baltimore, 1955). A model of monographic work covering state history is by Oscar Zeichner, *Connecticut's Years of Controversy* (Chapel Hill, 1949).

Several historians have dealt with the loyalists in exile. An early study is by Lewis Einstein, *Divided Loyalties: Americans in England during the War of Independence* (Boston, 1933). A work that concentrates upon loyalist claims, is by Wallace Brown, *The King's Friends* (Providence, Rhode Island, 1965). In conjunction with Brown, however, one should read the article by Eugene R. Fingerhut, "Uses and Abuses of the American Loyalist's Claims," *William and Mary Quarterly* (April, 1968), pp. 245–58. There are also several studies of loyalist plans for American reconciliation with Great Britain. One of the best is by Julian P. Boyd, *Anglo-American Union: Joseph Galloway's Plans to Preserve the British Empire* (Philadelphia, 1941). A more recent finding of what the author calls "one of the most enlightened Loyalist commentaries on the problem of governing America," is in Mary B. Norton, "John Randolph's 'Plan of Accommodation,'" *William and Mary Quarterly* (January, 1971), pp. 103–20.

Strangely enough, for all the historical attention devoted to the loyalists, there are few first-rate biographical studies of American Tories. Aubrey Land's book, previously mentioned, *The Dulanys of Maryland,* is outstanding; so is the work of Lawrence H. Gipson, *Jared Ingersoll* (New Haven, 1920). But we need modern biographies of, for example, Thomas Hutchinson and Peter Van Schaack as well as of other leading Tories.

Nineteenth-century historians were usually unsympathetic if not distinctly hostile to the loyalists. An exception is Lorenzo Sabine, *Biographical Sketches of Loyalists* (Boston, 1864). Though written frankly from a Whig persuasion, Sabine's study is remarkably well balanced. Also noteworthy is the treatment in Moses C. Tyler's *Literary History of the American Revolution* (New York, 1897), 2 volumes. Claude H. Van Tyne's volume, *The Loyalists in the American Revolution* (New York, 1902), though widely used, is a rather pedestrian effort. Some of the best writing on American loyalists in more recent years—by Leonard W. Labaree, Paul H. Smith, L. F. S. Upton, Wallace Brown, and William A. Benton—is included in this volume. The student should also consult an excellent work by William H. Nelson, *The American Tory* (Oxford, 1961), Wallace Brown's new volume, *The Good Americans: The Loyalists in the American Revolution* (New York, 1969), and Max Savelle's article, "Nationalism and Other Loyalties in the American Revolution," originally published in *The American Historical Review* and reprinted in Savelle's *Is Liberalism Dead?* (Seattle, 1967), pp. 97–126.

Finally, a significant aspect of the loyalist experience in America has been curiously neglected. There is no modern, sophisticated account of how the loyalists were treated: the various laws and loyalty oaths that were passed, especially those referring to "neutral and equivocal characters," their application, and the contrasts in punishment from state to state, as well as the contrasts in punishment before, during, and after the war.

# Index

# GREAT LIVES OBSERVED

Gerald Emanuel Stearn, *General Editor*

Other volumes in the series:

**(continued on following page)**

(continued from previous page)

Huey Long, *edited by Hugh Davis Graham*

Mao, *edited by Jerome Ch'en*

Joseph R. McCarthy, *edited by Allen J. Matusow*

Peter the Great, *edited by L. Jay Oliva*

Robespierre, *edited by George Rudé*

Franklin Delano Roosevelt, *edited by Gerald D. Nash*

Theodore Roosevelt, *edited by Dewey W. Grantham*

Stalin, *edited by T. H. Rigby*

Denmark Vesey: The Slave Conspiracy of 1822, *edited by*
  *Robert S. Starobin*

Booker T. Washington, *edited by Emma Lou Thornbrough*

George Washington, *edited by Morton Borden*